MAKING WAVES

The New Penguin Course
Advisory Editor: Rachel Belgrave, MA

MAKING WAVES

COURSE BOOK 2

Mandy Loader

and

Shane Wilkinson

PENGUIN ENGLISH

Published by the Penguin Group
Penguin Books Ltd, 27 Wrights Lane, London W8 5TZ, England
Viking Penguin, a division of Penguin Books USA Inc.
375 Hudson Street, New York, New York 10014, USA
Penguin Books Australia Ltd, Ringwood, Victoria, Australia
Penguin Books Canada Ltd, 2801 John Street, Markham, Ontario, Canada L3R 1B4
Penguin Books (NZ) Ltd, 182–190 Wairau Road, Auckland 10, New Zealand
Penguin Books Ltd, Registered Offices: Harmondsworth, Middlesex, England

First published in 1991
10 9 8 7 6 5 4 3 2 1

The publishers make grateful acknowledgement to the following for permission to reproduce copyright photographs: page 2, A. Garrido, Barnaby's Picture Library, Scottish Tourist Board; page 9, Rupert Crew Ltd; page 20, Paul Erdhardt, Camera Press Ltd; page 26, Barnaby's Picture Library; NYS Commerce Department; page 27, Barnaby's Picture Library; page 28, Lucy Horne, Barnaby's Picture Library; David Simson, Barnaby's Picture Library; Daniel Gallon, French Tourist Office: page 39, Ivor Guest, Popperfoto; Gerald Clyde, Barnaby's Picture Library; page 40, British Airways; Barnaby's Picture Library; Bridgeman Art Library; page 43, Holiday Inn; Farming Information Centre, NFU; page 71, Jeremy Hartley/Oxfam; Newcastle Chronicle and Journal Ltd; page 74, Steve Richards; page 84, The Mansell Collection; page 91, The National Gallery; Arxiu Mas, Barcelona; page 95, © Royal Marines Commando Training Centre/Jill Saunderson; © Peter Hologate; page 99, The Bridgeman Art Library; Mary Evans Picture Library; page 104, Camera Press London; Popperfoto

Every effort has been made to trace copyright holders in every case. The publishers would be interested to hear from any not acknowledged here

Designed by DW Design Partnership Ltd
Photo research by Merilyn Thorold
Filmset in New Baskerville and Futura
Made and printed in Hong Kong

CONTENTS

COURSE STRUCTURE

STRUCTURE	TOPIC	FUNCTION	PRONUNCIATION
Unit 1 Revision of past simple, regular / irregular verbs	Holidays	Apologizing and responding	-*ed* ending
Unit 2 Past simple, time adverbials	Love stories	Expressing interest	Intonation of acknowledgements
Unit 3 *Must / mustn't,* *Needn't*	Smuggling	Requests	*Must*
Unit 4 Adjective modifiers	Food and restaurants	Critical judgements	Stress shift
Unit 5 Active review of past simple, regular and irregular verbs. Passive review of *when* clauses, noun clauses, modification of adjectives, *too / enough*. Introduction of *had to*.	Living dangerously		
Unit 6 Present continuous with future meaning	Leisure	Inviting, accepting, refusing	/ʊ:/
Unit 7 Comparative adjectives	Countries	Agreeing and disagreeing	Stress shift
Unit 8 Superlative adjectives	Shopping	Making a purchase	Prices – pence and pounds
Unit 9 Present perfect	Business	Suggestions	Present perfect contractions
Unit 10 Active review of present continuous with future meaning, comparative and superlative forms of adjectives, present perfect, invitations, refusing, accepting, agreeing and disagreeing, suggestions	Travel		
Unit 11 Present perfect contrasted with past simple	Interviews	Checking meanings	Question intonation
Unit 12 Quantifiers	Are you liberated?	Requests, offers, refusals, acceptances	Intonation of requests

* = *see Study Book*

LISTENING	READING	WRITING	SPEAKING	SELF-HELP
Informal conversation	Travel brochure, Story		Role-play, discussion	Language of instructions Keeping a vocabulary book Spelling rules *
Recorded personal information	Parallel story, Biography		Narrative, Discussion	Revising vocabulary *
Radio interview	Scanning news cuttings	Lists, Guided sentences	Discussion	
Mini-dialogues	Scanning advertisements		Group discussion, Negotiation	
Radio interview	Magazine articles	Guided note-taking	Discussion, Interview	Deducing meaning from context Using your dictionary *
Casual conversation		Dictation, Writing invitations	Making plans	Guided sentence writing
Discussion	Newspaper articles	Note-taking	Making comparisons	
Publicity talk, Mini-dialogues	Flow-charts	Shopping dictation	Role-play	Language of Instructions
Interviews	Reading notes	A business plan	Role-play	
Dialogues		Note-taking	Role-play	Using your dictionary *
Interviews	Curriculum vitae	Form-filling	Role-play	
Mini-dialogues	Questionnaire	Dictation	Discussion	Spelling

STRUCTURE	TOPIC	FUNCTION	PRONUNCIATION
Unit 13 Comparative adverbs	Learning languages	Encouragement	/eɪ /*(may)*
Unit 14 *If* + present simple + *should*	Superstitions	Giving and accepting advice	/uː/ *(choose)*
Unit 15 Active review of present perfect versus past simple, present perfect with ever / never, future simple for polite requests and offers, *should/should have*	Treasure		
Unit 16 First conditional	Dreams	Offers	Intonation of exclamations
Unit 17 *Can / could*	Politeness	Permission	Intonation of permission
Unit 18 Linking words	The Third World	Asking and explaining	/ɜː/ *(work)*
Unit 19 Past continuous	Humour Jokes	Adverbials	/wɒz/ and /wəz/
Unit 20 Active review of first conditional, *can* (ability, permission, request), *could / may* (requests), linking words, past continuous, explanations, exclamations, offers	The good language learner		
Unit 21 *Used to*	Upstairs / downstairs	Expressing interest	Fall-rise intonation
Unit 22 Multi-word verbs	Banking	Filling in forms	Saying numbers
Unit 23 *May / might*	Fine art	Expressing doubt and uncertainty	Stress / intonation
Unit 24 *Make / let*	Commando!	Interruptions	Interruptions
Unit 25 Active review of *used to, may / might*, multi-word verbs, expressing interest / doubt, interrupting, coping	Haunted!		

LISTENING	READING	WRITING	SPEAKING	SELF-HELP
Informal discussion	Multiple-choice questionnaire	Questionnaire questions	Discussion	
Informal conversation	Horoscopes	Messages from an answer-phone	Describing superstitions, Discussion	Using your dictionary *
Reports	Jigsaw	Dictation	Discussion	Writing
Radio interview	Book extract	Radio review	Role-play	Maximizing learning
Informal dialogue	Magazine article	Postcard	Guided dialogues	Learning about grammar *
A speech	Brochure	Notes	Role-play	Spelling, Learning about grammar *
Humourous story	Story	Guided story writing	Discussion, Story-telling	
Dialogue	Article on learning			Using your dictionary *
Informal discussion	Biographies	Notes	Discussion	Learning about grammar *
Formal dialogue	Short newspaper stories	A bank form	Discussion	Deducing meaning
Mini-dialogues	Art catalogue Story	Describing pictures	Guided dialogues	Learning about grammar *
Press interview	Diary	Diary	Discussion	Spelling
Dialogue	Stories	Guided ghost story	Discussion, Story-telling	

STRUCTURE	TOPIC	FUNCTION	PRONUNCIATION
Unit 26 *-ing* form *so / neither*	Eccentrics	Sharing opinions and experience	Intonation
Unit 27 Relative clauses	General knowledge quizzes	Exclamations	Intonation of exclamations
Unit 28 Reported speech	TV and films	Describing with adjectives	/ɪ/ and /iː/
Unit 29 Question tags	Justice	Checking information	Intonation
Unit 30 Active review of relative clauses, verbs of liking + gerund, reported speech, question tags, exclamations, *so / (n)either / too*, summing up with adjectives, checking information.	Getting rich quickly		

LISTENING	READING	WRITING	SPEAKING	SELF-HELP
Group discussion	Book extracts	Newspaper article	Interviews	
Mini-dialogues	A quiz	Quiz questions	Role-play	Mnemonics, remembering words
The news	Film reviews	Dictation	Discussion	
Courtroom hearing	Police statement	Report	Role-play	Learning about grammar *
Lecture	Magazine article	Guided sentence Writing	Discussion	Mnemonics, remembering words

UNIT 1

PART A

START UP

Look at the pictures.

Work in pairs.

What sort of holidays do the pictures show?

A **Write words in the balloons to describe different kinds of holidays.**

B **Look at the diagram, and choose your three favourite types of holiday. Underline them.**

C **Compare your favourite holidays with your partner's.**

1 When did you have these holidays?
2 Who did you go with?

D **Talk to each other about your last holiday.**

Where did you go and what did you do?

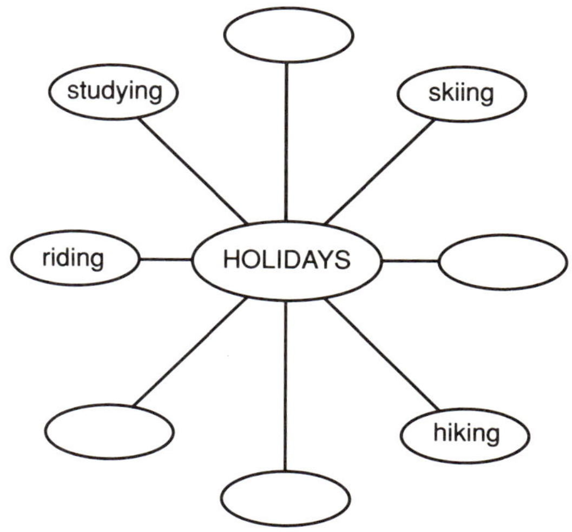

Grammar Guide

The Past Tense

Events: *She went to Spain last year.*
Situations: *She stayed in a beautiful hotel.*
Actions: *She visited lots of famous sites.*

There are two kinds of verbs – regular and irregular.

Regular verbs do not change their stem, but they add an ending:

Stem	+	**Ending**	=	**Past form**
walk	+	*ed*	=	*walked*
live	+	*d*	=	*lived*
carry (-y)	+	*ied*	=	*carried*
step (+p)	+	*ed*	=	*stepped*

One very common irregular verb is the verb *be*. The past tense is formed like this:

I	*am*	–	*was/wasn't*	*We*	*are*	–	*were/weren't*
You	*are*	–	*were/weren't*	*You*	*are*	–	*were/weren't*
He/she/it	*is*	–	*was/wasn't*	*They*	*are*	–	*were/weren't*

PRONUNCIATION

Regular verb endings in the past tense can be pronounced in three ways, /t/, /d/, or /ɪd/.

Listen to the tape.

You will hear examples of the three different pronunciations.

Listen to the examples, and then fill in below.

1 /t/ (kicked) **2** /d/ (loved) **3** /ɪd/ (wanted)

LISTENING

Look at the information in the travel brochure. Listen to Mr and Mrs Smith talking to their friends about their holiday.

1 Two weeks in sunny Spain for only £330.00.
2 Quiet, family hotel on beach.
3 Full board – three delicious meals a day.
4 Bathrooms with every room.
5 Fun and games for children.
6 Beautiful swimming pool.
7 Sightseeing tours every day.
8 Free windsurfing.
9 Transfers to and from airport.
10 Bar open twenty-four hours.
11 All inclusive – no extras to pay.

1 Which information in the brochure was wrong?
2 How was it wrong?
3 What other problems did the family have?
4 Do you think they enjoyed their holiday?

PRACTICE

Look at the pictures, which show some of the problems the family had.

Fill the gaps in the sentences with the verbs below. Use the past tense.

Some of the verbs are irregular.

leave stay arrive get be enjoy
want cost wait lie

1 The Smith family were tired when they __________ . They __________ for the bus till one o'clock.
2 The taxi __________ £40.00 and Mr Smith __________ his wallet in the taxi.
3 There __________ no water in the swimming pool.
4 The children __________ on the beach and __________ sunburnt.
5 They didn't __________ the sightseeing tours.
6 Mr and Mrs Smith __________ to leave after a week, but the flights were full, so they __________

DEVELOPMENT

In groups of three, talk about a holiday you had when things went wrong.

What went wrong, why, and what did you do about it?

VOCABULARY

Across

1 A means of transport. (5)
4 On holiday, you want the weather to be __________ .(4)
6 Before you go, it's wise to __________ a hotel room. (4)
8 If you're hiking, you carry a __________ on your back. (8)
10 If the sea is warm, you can __________ .(4)
12 The water's not shallow, it's __________ .(4)
13 It doesn't cost much to __________ a boat for an hour.(4)
14 If you're camping, don't forget your __________ ! (4)

Down

1 He did a one-week __________ of the country. (4)
2 I'm staying __________ the Riviera Hotel. (2)
3 The opposite of quiet. (5)
4 Accommodation which includes all meals. (4,5)
5 I'd like to __________ a booking, please.(4)
7 I like empty beaches, I hate __________ ones. (7)
9 I'm very __________ windsurfing. (4,2)
11 A place to stay if you're touring. (5)

START UP

PART B

In the UK, people apologize very often. The cartoon shows a woman apologizing.

1 Why is she apologizing ?
2 What sort of things do people apologize for?
3 Do people apologize very often in your country?

Function Focus

Apologies

Look at these different ways of apologizing and replying.

I'm sorry.	*That's OK.*
Oh dear, I'm sorry.	*It's all right.*
I'm really very sorry.	*Never mind.*
I'm very sorry.	*It doesn't matter.*
I'm so sorry.	*Don't worry about it.*
I'm terribly sorry.	*Well, don't do it again!*
I am sorry.	*That's quite all right.*

LISTENING

Listen to Mr Smith talking to a travel agent.

Mr Smith is complaining about the holiday they had in Spain.

1 How many times does the travel agent apologize?
2 Which of the phrases listed in the Function Focus does she use?

DEVELOPMENT

In pairs, finish the conversation. One of you is Mr Smith, the other is the travel agent. Don't forget to talk about everything that went wrong.

PRACTICE

When we apologize, we usually say why we are apologizing.

	your room was noisy.
I'm very sorry	*the hotel was dirty.*
	I forgot your birthday.
	I was late for your party.

A Look at these pictures.

John is staying with his friend Peter, but everything is going wrong. John is very unlucky.

a

b

c

d

Match the pictures on page 4 to these sentences.

1 John burnt the dinner.
2 He borrowed Peter's pen and lost it.
3 He spilt coffee all over the carpet.
4 He broke Peter's tennis racquet.

B In pairs, imagine you are John and Peter in the situations the pictures show. Apologize and reply .

Example:
John *Oh dear. I'm sorry I burnt the dinner.*
Peter *It doesn't matter.*

C Now think of other things John did and apologized for. Use the following ideas to help you. Your partner will reply.

Example:
break/bicycle

John *I'm terribly sorry I broke your bicycle.*
Peter *Never mind.*

be late/lunch *forget/birthday*
break/cassette player *lose/dictionary*

READING

This is a true story. Below are four possible titles for the story.

A Read the titles.

1 An Expensive Dinner
2 Noodles and Cabbage Again!
3 A Difficult Situation
4 A Delicious Meal

What do you think the story will be about?

B Read the story, and decide which of the titles is the best one for this story. Compare your answer with your partner's.

We were on holiday in Scandinavia. We were camping and we had very little money. Every night we had noodles and cabbage, and on Sundays a tin of tuna. One evening, we went into a café for a cup of coffee. A man was having dinner at the table next to us. It looked wonderful. He had a huge plate of meat and vegetables, a big glass of orange juice, some bread and butter and a bowl of pudding. We sat and talked over our coffee.

Suddenly, the man got up and left. He had only eaten a little of his huge dinner. We stared at it for five minutes. We were very hungry. At last, I went over to his table, picked up his food and put it down on our table. We shared it out. It was delicious! At last we finished it, and sat back happily. Just then the door opened and the man came back...

C In groups of three:

1 Talk about a holiday you had with very little money. What did you do?
2 Think of a good ending for this story. Tell your ending to the rest of the class.

SELF-HELP

In the instructions for the exercises, you will find these words:

1 appropriate
2 the following
3 verb stem
4 regular verb
5 irregular verb
6 compare

If you are not sure what these words mean, match them to the definitions below:

a To look at something and see what is the same and what is different
b Verbs which end in *-ed* in the past simple, for example, walk – walk*ed*, look – look*ed*.
c The next.
d Verbs which change their stem to make the past simple, for example, *go – went, eat – ate.*
e The basic form of the verb, for example, *go, look, walk, eat.*
f Right, suitable.

VOCABULARY BANK

To be/go on holiday.
The *travel agent* is the person who *books* the flights and organizes *transfers* from the airport to the hotel.
Travel *brochures* give information about holidays.
Sightseeing tours are a good way of seeing the country.
If you don't want to sightsee with other people, you can *rent* a car and *tour* by yourself.
You *apologize* if you lose your friend's pen.
Verbs *stems* are the basic form of the verb.

UNIT 2

PART A

START UP

This picture illustrates a story.

1 What kind of story does the picture illustrate?
2 Do you enjoy love stories?
3 What famous love stories do you know?

Grammar Guide

Time Adverbials

Adverbial Clause	Main Clause
When she arrived	*I stood up*

Main Clause	Adverbial Clause
I stood up	*when she arrived*

These are some common time adverbials which we use in adverbial clauses.

when *before* *after* *as soon as*

PRACTICE 1

Join these sentences using the time adverbials in the Grammar Guide.

1 She met him.	She was lonely.
2 She saw him.	She fell in love with him.
3 They got married.	They went on a honeymoon.
4 They arrived in Spain.	They began to argue.
5 They got there.	The hotel was fully booked.
6 They returned from their honeymoon.	Things got better.

READING

Work in pairs.

Student 1 Read the first part of the story.
Student 2 Read the second part.

Do not read the other part of the story. Then put your books down, and tell each other the story, starting with Student 1.

Student 1
As soon as he heard the phone ring, John remembered. The disco!
It was his friend Peter.
'Is that you, John? What are you doing? You're late! It's 9.30 and I'm waiting!'
'Peter, I'm really sorry but I forgot – there was something really good on television.'
'Well, never mind, it's not too late. Can you come and get me now?'
'OK, I'll be there in five minutes.'
John ran out of the house and got into his car. He went to Peter's house and then they drove to the disco. They went inside.
The room was crowded and noisy although it was only 10 o'clock. Peter bought drinks at the bar while John found a couple of seats by the dance floor. And then it happened. The moment John saw her, he knew it was love at first sight.

Student 2
The moment John saw her, he knew it was love at first sight. She came slowly into the room, and looked round. Her hair was long, the colour of the sun, and her eyes were the colour of the sea on a summer's day.
He turned to his friend Peter.
'She's the most beautiful girl in the world,' he said.
'Well, good luck,' he replied, 'she's not my type. I'll see you later.'
He went off to talk to some friends. John was alone. He looked at the girl until she turned round. When she saw him, she smiled. John hesitated and then stood up. He crossed the room. Their eyes met.
'Hello,' he said, 'I'm John.'
'Hello,' she replied. 'I'm Alex. Who's that lovely guy you were with? Can you introduce us?'

PRACTICE 2

The following time adverbials occur in the story:
as soon as *while* *the moment* *until* *when*

Complete the following sentences. Use the adverbials as appropriate.

The first has been done for you

1 *As soon as he heard the phone ring,* John remembered. The disco!

2 Peter bought the drinks ____________ seats.
3 ____________ he knew it was love at first sight.
4 He looked at the girl ____________ round.
5 ____________ , she smiled.

Now write the last sentence, using the adverbial *after*.

START UP

PART B

A famous pop group once said 'All you need is love'.

Look at the six balloons. They each contain a famous saying about love. Now look at the six boxes. Match the boxes to the balloons.

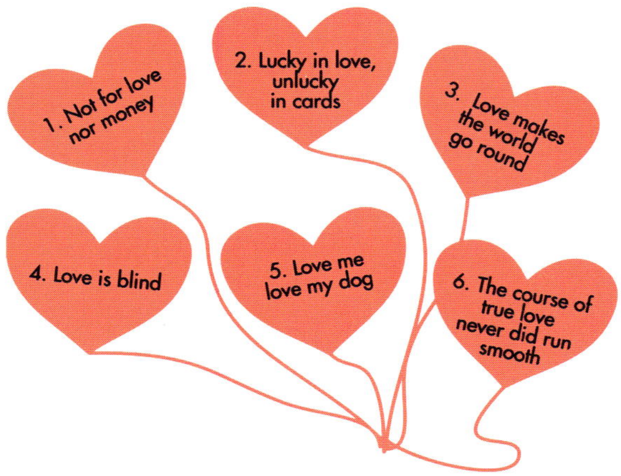

a Life is easier with love.

b People in love don't see clearly.

c If you love me, accept me as I am.

d If you win women, you'll lose at cards.

e True love has ups and downs.

f Not for anything.

What sayings about love do you have in your language?

Translate them into English and tell them to the class.

Function Focus

Showing Interest

We show our interest in what people are saying to us like this:

I'm an accountant.	*(Oh) are you?*
She lived in Paris.	*(Oh) did she?*
He's looking for a wife.	*(Oh) is he?*
She's only thirty.	*(Oh) really?*

PRONUNCIATION

Listen to the following information and show your interest.

Listen to the three examples.

LISTENING

Henry Dowd is the Director of a small English Language school. Henry is forty-three years old and unmarried, but he wants a wife. He went to a computer dating agency, and gave this information about himself:

Character: quiet and serious.
Likes: reading, going to the cinema, gardening, spaghetti and going to bed early.
Hobbies: listening to classical music, keeping goldfish and collecting stamps.
Height: one metre sixty-three centimetres.

A In pairs, discuss.

1 Do you think computer dating agencies are a good thing?
2 What do you think is the best way of meeting people?
3 What sort of woman is right for Henry Dowd?

B The agency gave Henry Dowd video tapes about four women.

Listen to the information and complete the chart below.

Name	Suzy	Elizabeth	Jessie	Petula	Your partner
Age	28				
Job		manager			
Height			1.66m		
Hobbies				eating foreign food	
Recent history					
Any other information					

C **Now listen to the cassette again, and match the two columns below.**

The first has been done for you.

1 Suzy lived in Paris (f)	**a** not long ago
2 Elizabeth got divorced	**b** recently
3 She doesn't have much time for hobbies	**c** last year
4 She got promoted	**d** nowadays
5 Jessie made a video	**e** the year before last
6 She recorded her first album	**f** until a year ago
7 Petula toured the world	**g** last month
8 She visited five different countries	**h** a few months ago

PRACTICE 1

What questions do you think the agent asked in order to obtain this information from her clients?

Look at the chart again. In pairs, imagine that one of you is the agent, and the other the client. Interview each other, and fill in the blank column 'Your partner' in the chart.

DEVELOPMENT 1

Which of the four women is the best wife for Henry Dowd?

Underline her name, and compare your answer with your partner's.

Do you agree? Why? Why not?

PRACTICE 2

Read about the life of Barbara Cartland.

She is one of the world's most famous love-story writers.

Use these words to fill the gaps.

a a few years ago
b shortly after
c after
d since then
e as soon as
f when

Barbara Cartland, love-story writer and TV personality, was born at the beginning of the century. She wrote her first book (1) __________ she was twenty-one and it sold out (2) __________ it reached the shops. (3) __________ she has written over 500 books, all about love. She married in 1927, and (4) __________ she divorced her first husband, she remarried in 1936. In 1976, she wrote twenty-one books and broke the world record, and (5) __________ this she sang an album of love songs with the Royal Philharmonic Orchestra. She continued to write, and (6) __________ became one of the world's top-selling writers. Some of her many titles include *Love Me For Ever, Love is Dangerous, Love is the Enemy* and *The Ghost Who Fell in Love.* She lives in the country near London.

DEVELOPMENT 2

In groups, discuss the following questions:

1 Why do people read love stories?
2 What are the names of famous writers of love stories in your country?
3 What sort of stories do you like reading?
4 Who is your favourite story writer?

VOCABULARY BANK

A lot of *marriages* end in *divorce.*
My sister is *married,* but my brother is *unmarried.*
As soon as he saw her, he *fell in love* with her.
When she saw him, she smiled.
He waited *while* she said good-bye to her mother.
He *introduced* her to his best friend.
Barbara Cartland is a *writer* of love *stories.*

UNIT
3

PART A

START UP

1 What is a smuggler?
2 Think of ten things people can smuggle.

US Customs Catch Heroin Smuggler

It was 11.30 p.m. at the Customs House between the United States and Mexico. A 1970 Dodge Sedan drove up slowly, and stopped. Mike Macormic, the customs officer at work that night, told me:

'The driver had nothing to declare but I put the car's number into the computer. I do that for all cars from Mexico. The driver of the car waited quietly. I looked at the computer. Suddenly, I saw the word: HIT! That meant the driver was a smuggler. Right, I thought, now I must find what he's hiding.'

Mr Macormic asked the driver to get out of the car. He began to search it.

'I took out the seats, then I looked in the engine for hiding places. The driver smoked while I searched his car. Then, after two hours, I began to check the roof. The moment I touched it, the driver ran off towards Mexico. I ran after him, caught him and brought him back.'

Mr Macormic later found 11 kilograms of heroin inside the roof.

READING 1

Read this newspaper story and look at the pictures.

They illustrate the story, but they are not in the right order.

Put them in the right order by writing the letters b–d in the correct box.

The first one has been done for you.

WRITING

In pairs:

A Mike is new to his job as a customs officer. This is the list of smuggled goods he is making to help him in his work.

Complete his list for him.

Smuggled Goods

1. Watch.
2. Gold.
3.

B Mike is also making a list of hiding-places for smuggled goods.

Do it for him. Write 'Hiding-places' at the top of the list, and think of ten hiding-places. Number them 1–10.

Grammar Guide

Must* and *Needn't

Must and *Needn't* are modal auxiliary verbs, which we use with other verbs.

Must means: It's the law or it's necessary.

Example:
*You **must** go through customs when you enter a foreign country.*
*You **mustn't** smuggle drugs.*

Needn't means: It's not the law or it's not necessary.

Example:
*You **needn't declare** ten cigarettes.*

Affirmative	Negative	Interrogative
Pronoun + *must* + verb	Pronoun + *Mustn't* + verb	*Must* + pronoun + verb?
I must go.	*I mustn't stay.*	*Must you go?*
	Pronoun + *needn't* + verb	

PRONUNCIATION

Listen to the cassette and practise the pronunciation of *must*.

READING 2

A **Read the following questions and then look at the Customs leaflet. Write the answers in your notebook.**

Note: An allowance is something you needn't declare.

1 What must you declare when you enter the UK?
2 You want to bring a knife into the UK. What must you do?
3 What needn't you declare?
4 You have 1 litre of spirits. Must you declare it?

Anything to Declare?

Your Allowances

You needn't declare:
1 litre spirits or 2 litres fortified or sparkling wine
2 litres still table wine
60 millilitres perfume
250 millilitres toilet water
£32 worth of gifts and souvenirs
200 cigarettes or 50 cigars

Goods to Declare

You must declare:
anything more than your allowances
anything prohibited

Prohibited Goods.

You must declare:
drugs: heroin, cocaine, cannabis
guns, knives, explosives
meat, chicken, eggs and milk
plants, fruit, vegetables
animals and birds.
Note: All live animals must go into quarantine

B **In pairs, ask your partner more questions like the ones above the customs leaflet.**

PRACTICE

A **In pairs, look at these suitcases. Ask and answer questions about the things in the cases.**

Example:
Suitcase 1:
*What **must** I declare?*
*You **must** declare the whisky, but you **needn't** declare the wine.*

1 2

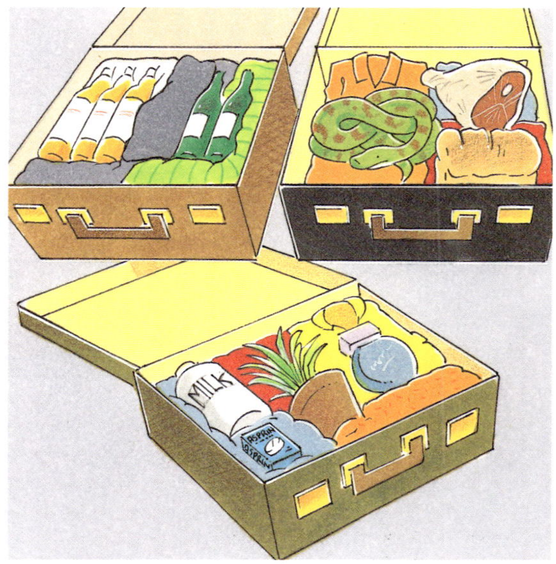

3

B The book *Trucker's Bible* gives advice about how to smuggle.

It says:

You mustn't avoid the customs officer's eyes.
You mustn't behave unnaturally.

What other advice do you think it gives?

In pairs, write sentences using *mustn't*.

C **Write more sentences, this time as a customs officer. Use the two pictures below to help you.**

Example:
*You **mustn't** lie to the customs officer!*

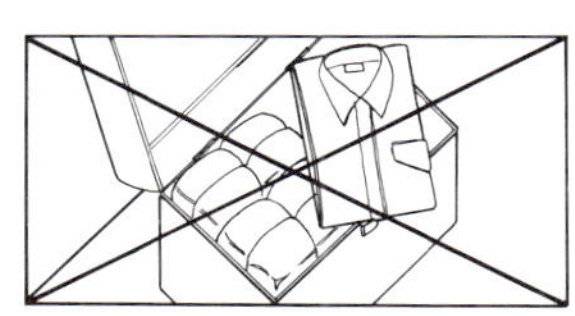

START UP

PART B

This is called a wordsearch. Seven words from the story are hidden in the box. The words can go across from right to left, down or in this direction ↘. The first letter of each word is grey.

Draw a line around all the words that you find.

The first one has been done for you.

K	D	Z	F	T	A	B	G	D	O	R	J	L	H
Q	K	A	T	V	K	E	V	E	G	P	X	M	I
E	F	I	N	D	W	F	N	U	M	N	U	C	D
T	G	D	L	J	H	S	U	I	T	C	A	S	E
F	C	F	O	M	K	R	M	A	M	F	B	R	Q
B	U	P	D	R	E	G	H	U	H	B	M	R	A
F	S	F	Z	L	T	I	D	R	G	H	E	K	G
H	T	K	S	E	A	R	C	H	V	G	N	R	J
N	O	A	T	Y	R	F	H	D	E	R	L	S	C
F	M	A	O	V	B	H	E	A	T	A	I	E	B
W	S	G	P	B	D	S	C	X	W	D	N	B	R

Function Focus

Requests with *Could* and *Can*

We use *could* and *can* to make requests. They have the same meaning.

Can	*for a friend* *for someone in your family*
Could	*for someone you don't know* *for someone you know a little*

You sometimes hear these requests at the Customs:

Request	Response
Could *you open your suitcase , please.*	*Yes of course.*
Could *you show me your handbag, please.*	*Yes certainly.*
Could *you follow me, please.*	*OK.*
Could *I see your passport, please.*	*Yes of course.*

PRACTICE

Here are some requests that you hear:

a in a restaurant
b in a shop
c at home

A Read them and decide whether the request belongs to group *a*, *b*, or *c*.

1 Could you bring me the menu, please?
2 This watch doesn't work. Could you change it, please?
3 Can you tidy your room, please?
4 Could I have the bill, please?
5 Can you help me with my homework, please?
6 Could you show me a smaller size, please?

B In pairs, make requests and responses from these prompts:

1 You're lost. You want to go to the station. What do you say to a policeman?
2 You want to complain to the manager about a bad holiday. What do you say to the travel agent?
3 You want to dance with a person you see in the disco. What do you say to him/her?
4 You want your friend to post a letter for you. What do you say to her?
5 It's crowded but there's an empty seat next to an old lady. What do you say to her?

WRITING

Write more some examples of requests. Choose requests you hear in other situations. Show them to your partner. Your partner must guess which situation the request belongs to.

LISTENING

These smugglers are carrying their goods themselves. But it's dangerous. If they can, smugglers get other people to smuggle for them.

They often choose old people and children for this because the customs do not usually search them.

Sometimes people do not know they are carrying smuggled goods.

Listen to these true stories and complete the chart.

	Teresa and Lynn	Sid and Nancy Gill
Ages		
Country visited		
Length of stay		
Where arrested		
Smuggled goods		
Hiding-place		
What happened to them		

DEVELOPMENT

In groups, discuss the following questions:

1. Did a customs officer ever search you? Did he find anything?
2. Is smuggling a serious crime?
3. What stories do you know about smugglers and smuggling?

VOCABULARY BANK

Smugglers sometimes *hide* goods in very clever hiding-places.

Customs officers search people to *find smuggled goods.*

You *must* declare any animals you bring into the country.

You mustn't *smuggle* goods into the country.

UNIT 4

PART A

START UP

The Prince of India – for a really hot, spicy vindaloo or for mild, delicately flavoured curries. *take-away service*open until midnight.

69, High Street, Poole. Tel: 676330

La Mamma – excellent pizzas and pastas*nice atmosphere*a good wine list*very low prices.

100 Wimborne Road. Bournemouth. Tel: 515208

McDonald's Hamburgers – pretty fast and pretty good food. Open seven days a week* parking space.

554 Christchurch Road. Tel: 35877

The Peking Duck – superb Peking cuisine. Parties welcome*take away service*we specialise in Peking Duck.

234 Holdenhurst Road. Tel: 23748

Le Sanglier qui Fume – for the perfect romantic French meal by candlelight. *full à la carte menu *dinner dances*telephone for reservations.

73 Haven Road, Poole. Tel. 707272

The Olde English Kitchen – extremely good traditional English cooking. Ideal for business lunches*weddings and special occasions*roast Sunday lunches for the family.

91 Palmerston Road. Tel: 36074

In pairs, look at these advertisements for different kinds of restaurants. Talk about each one.

1 What kind of food do they serve?
2 Do you like that kind of food. Why? Why not?
3 What is your favourite dish?

Grammar Guide

Adjective Modifiers

Modifiers are words which we use to make adjectives stronger or weaker.

Word Order:

Article +	Modifier +	Adjective +	Noun
A	*very*	*expensive*	*car*

Look at this:

*It's an **extremely***
*It's a **really*** *tasty soup*
*It's a **very***
*It's a **pretty*** *hot curry*
*It's a **fairly***

Exception: *quite*
We put *quite* before the article *(a/an)*.
Example:
*It's **quite** a hot curry*

However, there are some adjectives which are already strong, such as *delicious, revolting* and *disgusting*. We don't usually use *very* with these words.

For these adjectives you can:

1 Use them on their own.
2 Make them very strong, with words like *absolutely* and *really*.

Example:
*This soup is tasty. < This soup is **very** tasty.*
*This soup is very tasty! = This soup is **delicious!***
*This soup is delicious! < This soup is **absolutely** delicious!*

Too / Enough
When we don't like something the way it is, or we want to change it, we often use the words *too* and *enough* with the adjective.

Example:
*It's **too** spicy. (I can't eat it.)*
*It isn't spicy **enough.** (It needs more spices.)*

These sentences can also be modified.

Look at this chart:

It isn't quite spicy enough .
nearly

It's a bit too spicy.
much
far
miles

PRACTICE

Read the advertisements on page 14 again.

A Underline all the modifiers you can find.

B Put a circle around the following unmodified adjectives:

mild excellent good superb welcome perfect special

Think of a suitable modification for each one.

Example:
very mild or *quite mild.*

C The following pairs of sentences are mixed up. Match each sentence 1–10 with a sentence a–j.

The answer to the first one is 1d:

This soup is absolutely delicious. It's really tasty.

1 This soup is absolutely delicious.
2 That's a very fine teapot.
3 She's a fairly good cook.
4 I've found a pretty unusual cheese.
5 It's quite a nice cake.
6 This pear's absolutely rotten.
7 I've got a really tiny portion of food.
8 We need an absolutely enormous pan.
9 My knife is completely useless.
10 It's a pretty dreadful recipe.

a I've never had it before.
b I don't think I'll use it again.
c But she needs more practice.
d It's really tasty.
e It won't be enough for me.
f But it needs more sugar.
g I'm going to throw it away.
h It's absolutely beautiful.
i It won't fit in anything smaller.
j It won't cut anything.

D **Look at this conversation:**

Speaker 1 I don't like Chinese food. It's not salty enough. What do you think?

Speaker 2 I don't agree. I think it's too salty.

Now use these ideas to practise similar conversations with your partner.

Cola drinks – sweet *English beer – strong*
Indian curry – hot *Mediterranean oranges – juicy*
Chinese tea – strong

PRONUNCIATION

A If you emphasize adjective modifiers, you make their meaning stronger. We do this very often in English.

Listen to these comments.

Speaker 1 is the man, Speaker 2 is the woman. Which is being more emphatic?

Put a tick in the column of the more emphatic speaker.

The first two have been done for you.

	Man	Woman
1		✓
2		✓
3		
4		
5		
6		
7		
8		
9		
10		

B **Now listen to the comments again, and write them down. Practise saying them with a partner.**

Can you tell when your partner is emphasizing them?

START UP

Look at the picture and the saying about food.

PART B

Too many cooks spoil the broth.

(Broth is a thin soup.)

What sayings do you have in your language about food and cooking?

Talk about them with your partner.

Function Focus

Asking for Judgements

Here are some ways of asking people for their opinions or judgements.
What do you think of/about American food?
What is (What's) the food like in your country?
How is (How's) the weather in your country?

Making Critical Judgements

This is how you can reply to the questions:
I'd say it's ...
Well, I think it's ...
In my opinion, it's ...
It seems (to me) to be ...
Remember: you can use these phrases when talking about any subject.

PRACTICE

In pairs, ask for and give opinions about the following topics:

English pop music *French clothes*
English weather *German wine* *Italian food*
modern architecture *sports* *modern art*

VOCABULARY

Look at these words.

They are adjectives which describe food.

Think about the typical cooking of the countries listed. Choose an adjective which you think describes that country's cooking.

One has been done for you.

exotic ← →	Japan
heavy	
uninteresting	Germany
rich	Japan
plain	Italy
tasty	Britain
boring	Spain
delicious	Greece
spicy	Mexico
unhealthy	France
salty	
oily	

Compare your answers with your partner's.

Do you agree?

Remember to make critical judgements.

Example:

Well, I think the food in Britainis absolutely delicious.

Oh really? In my opinion, it's rather heavy.

LISTENING

Listen to the following six conversations.

In each conversation people are talking about food or drink.

Fill in the chart below.

The first one has been done for you.

	1	2	3	4	5	6
Kind of food/ drinks	*Sangria*					
The problem	*not sweet enough*					
What to do	*add more sugar*					

DEVELOPMENT

A What kinds of food and drink do you enjoy making and eating?

Describe your favourites to your partner.

What kind of food don't you like?

B **In groups of four, imagine you are going out for a meal with the whole class. Look at the advertisements for the different kinds of restaurants at the beginning of the unit.**

Which do you think would be the best restaurant to go to?

After your group decides, compare your decision with the other groups. Persuade the whole class that your decision is the best.

Here are some examples of what you can say:

1 Well, I think French food is too expensive – I'm not rich enough.
2 I think hamburgers are boring but Indian food is too hot.
3 Japanese food is exotic, but it's not sweet enough.

VOCABULARY BANK

Chinese restaurants are *fairly* expensive.
I can't eat Indian food – it's *too spicy*.
I think French *cooking* is *extremely tasty*.
My favourite dish is spaghetti with tomato sauce – it's *delicious*!
My favourite kind of *food* is Italian.
Where shall we go for a *meal* tonight? Let's look at the *advertisements*.

UNIT 5

PART A

START UP

In pairs, look at the picture.

The boat is sinking.

1 Why is it sinking?
2 Why do boats usually sink?
3 What are the people doing?

Talk about other accidents at sea, for example, the sinking of the *Titanic*, the mystery of the *Marie Celeste*, or something that happened to you.

READING

Read the page from the boat's diary shown in the picture above. Now read the four paragraphs below. They are mixed up. Put the paragraphs in the right order:

1[ ] 2[ ] 3[ ] 4[ ]

a As soon as they saw it, they knew they were in trouble. They filled the hole with blankets, but that didn't stop the water coming in. Then they tried to cover the hole, but that didn't work, either.
b Maurice and Maralyn Bailey were on a trip round the world, by boat. They were in the Pacific, not far from the Galapagos Islands, when the accident happened. It was just after seven o'clock in the morning, and the weather was absolutely perfect.
c They had to leave their boat, and get into the raft. They felt totally helpless and completely alone.
d Suddenly, they felt a bang. They saw a whale in the water. They were terrified. Then the whale disappeared, but the boat began to go down. There was a big hole in the boat.

PRACTICE 1

A When the Baileys got back to England, a newspaper wanted their story. A reporter asked the Baileys a lot of questions. At the top of page 19 are the answers the Baileys gave. What were the questions that the reporter asked?

Complete the reporter's check-list of questions.

The first has been done for you.

List of questions about boat sinking.

1. What was the name of the boat?

2.

3.

1 The Auralyn.
2 Maurice and Maralyn Bailey.
3 In the Pacific, near the Galapagos Islands.
4 Seven o'clock.
5 Absolutely perfect.
6 Because of the hole.
7 We filled the hole with blankets.
8 Totally helpless and alone.

B The reporter did not write the Bailey's story correctly. Maurice made a note of all the mistakes. He then wrote and complained to the newspaper.

Read the newspaper story and complete Maurice's letter with six more points.

Boat Sinks in the Atlantic

Maurice and Maralyn Bailey came back to the UK last week. They were on a trip round the world, on their boat the Aurora. Then there was an accident. It happened at eleven o'clock. The weather was terrible. A whale hit their boat and holed it. They tried to fill the hole with towels. Their boat sank and they got into the raft. They were in a difficult situation, but they felt hopeful.

Dear Sir,
Please note the following mistakes in yesterday's article: Boat Sinks in the Atlantic.

1. The boat didn't sink in the Atlantic, it sank in the Pacific.

Yours faithfully, Maurice Bailey

Grammar Guide

The Past Form of *Must*

In Unit 3 we looked at *must*.
Now we will look at the past form of *must*.

Affirmative:	*They **had to** leave their boat.*
Negative:	*They **didn't have to** leave their boat.*
Interrogative:	***Did** they **have to** leave their boat?*

PRACTICE 2

A Use the following verbs to makes sentences about what the Baileys had to do after their boat sank. Use the pictures to help you.

The first has been done for you.

fight look for eat leave catch drink

1 They *had to leave their* boat.
2 ________________ fish.
3 ________________ rainwater.
4 ________________ sea birds.
5 ________________ sharks.
6 ________________ other boats.

B **In pairs, look at the pictures on page 19 again. Ask and answer questions:**

Example:
What did they have to drink?
They had to drink rainwater.

Think of other things they probably had to do, and tell the class.

DEVELOPMENT

When did you last have to do things you didn't want to do?

Tell your partner about your military service, your school, your job, or maybe when your car broke down or you didn't pass an exam.

What did you have to do, and why?

PART B

START UP

Look at the picture of white-water boating.

It's a dangerous sport.

1 What other sports are dangerous?
2 Do you enjoy any dangerous sports? Why? Why not?
3 What sports do you enjoy?

LISTENING

A This woman is talking about her first trip on white water for a radio programme about living dangerously. Did she enjoy herself?

B **Read these questions.**
Listen again, and put a tick ✔ as appropriate.

	Yes	No
1 Did they go on the water on the first day?		
2 Was the weather sunny and warm?		
3 Did they have to tie everything into the boats?		
4 Was the river slow at the beginning of the trip?		
5 Did she feel calm in the white water?		
6 Did her boat turn over?		
7 Was anybody killed?		
8 Did she want to go boating in white water again?		

C **Now listen to the tape again, and answer the following questions by putting a tick beside the correct answer.**

1 Did this story happen:
   a two years ago
   b a couple of weeks ago
   c last month
2 How many people were there?
   a eighteen
   b eight
   c eighty
3 The first night, she felt:
   a calm
   b nervous
   c very nervous
4 At the beginning, the river was:
   a slow
   b very fast
   c fast
5 When she went into the rough water she felt:
   a excited
   b happy
   c terrified

READING

A **Work in pairs.**

Student 1 Read the first part of this article.
Student 2 Read the second part.

Then close your books, and tell your part of the story to your partner, beginning with Student 1.

Life and Death on Everest

Student 1

Mount Everest is the highest mountain in the world.
In 1972, Chris Bonington tried to climb the south-west side but it was too cold and the winds were too strong. Before he left Kathmandu at the end of November 1972, Chris Bonington booked the mountain for another try. (Everest is an extremely popular mountain. You have to book your climb years in advance.) In 1975, he tried again. He chose his team very carefully. He asked Doug Scott and Dougal Haston to be members of his team. They made their camp at the bottom of the mountain in August, and then started to go up the mountain. One of the team fell ill, and he had to leave the mountain. The rest of the team continued to climb. They had to hurry to get to the top before the weather changed.

Student 2

On the 24 September, Doug Scott and Dougal Haston tried to get to the top of Everest. They felt very well in Camp 6, the highest camp on the mountain. The night before the climb, they drank tea and had supper. They discussed what to take with them to the top. They decided to leave their sleeping bags and tents behind because they were too heavy. At 2.30 a.m. they had breakfast, and got dressed. At 3.30 a.m. they began to climb. It was extremely difficult. The snow was very deep. After a long, hard fight they reached the top together. They laughed, shouted and took some photographs. It was sunny and the shadow of Everest was 300 kilometres long. Then the sun disappeared and the two men realized they were on the top of Everest and it was almost night. Camp 6 was too far to reach. They went a little way down the mountain, but there was no moon and it was too dangerous. They had to spend the night on the mountain, at 9,566 metres, with no tents, sleeping bags, or food. They believed it was possible. They made a hole in the snow, and climbed into it. They did not sleep. It was -30°C. When the light came at last they climbed down, and reached Camp 6. They talked to Chris Bonington by radio. Everybody was happy. The next little group prepared to climb to the top. Their story did not have a happy end. One man, Mick Burke, didn't come down. No one knows how he died.

B **Now read the other part of the article, and mark these statements true or false with a tick.**

		T	F
1	Chris Bonington climbed to the top of Everest in 1972.		
2	He went back to Everest in 1974.		
3	One man had to leave the expedition because of illness.		
4	Scott and Haston forgot their sleeping bags when they climbed to the top.		
5	They got to the top of Everest very late.		
6	It was cloudy at the top.		
7	There was a moon when they climbed down.		
8	They slept in a snow-hole.		
9	Chris Bonington was in Camp 6 when they arrived.		

DEVELOPMENT

In pairs, imagine one of you is the climber Doug Scott or Dougal Haston. The other is a reporter from a newspaper. Interview the climber.
Take notes under the following headings:
The Weather *The Climb* *At the Top*
Getting Down

SELF-HELP

When you see a word you do not understand, don't immediately pick up your dictionary! First, try to guess the meaning from the whole sentence. Try to guess the meaning of these nonsense words:

1 He sat on the gromble and drank his tea.
A gromble is a:
a person **b** chair **c** cup

2 She spegged the car to the station.
To speg is to:
a tie **b** climb **c** drive

3 It began to gollop so they ran into the house.
To gollop is to :
a rain **b** fight **c** sink

4 The wimble was quite delicious
A wimble is a:
a pen **b** meal **c** boat

5 A nonsense word is:
a an unusual word **b** a word with no meaning
c a difficult word

VOCABULARY BANK

There was an *accident*, and the *boat* sank, so they *had* to get into the raft.
Some people in the boat were a little *nervous* when they hit the white water. Most of them were *terrified*.
They had to *tie* their things into the boat.
When you *climb* a high mountain, you do it in a *team* of several people.

UNIT
6

PART A

START UP

In pairs, discuss the following questions:

1 Do you like speaking on the 'phone?
2 How often do you use a 'phone?
3 Do you most often use it for business, friendly calls, or invitations?
4 What are the disadvantages of telephones?

Grammar Guide

Future Time

There are many different ways of talking about the future.
We use the present continuous when we are talking about:
1 The near future.
2 Plans which are definite.

Do you remember how to form the present continuous tense?
Here it is again:

Affirmative

Subject	+ auxiliary	+ verb + *ing*
I	*am*	
We/you/they	*are*	*working*
He/she/it	*is*	

Interrogative

Auxiliary	+ subject	+ verb + *ing*
Am	*I*	
Are	*we/you/they*	*working*
Is	*he/she/it*	

Here are two examples of the present continuous tense used for expressing the future:

(It is 2 o'clock)
Speaker 1 *Are you leaving at four o'clock?*
Speaker 2 *No, I'm leaving at five.*

Speaker 1 *How are you getting to France tomorrow?*
Speaker 2 *I'm driving.*

WRITING

These pictures tell a story. You can hear the same story on the cassette.

Listen to the dialogue and write the words you hear.

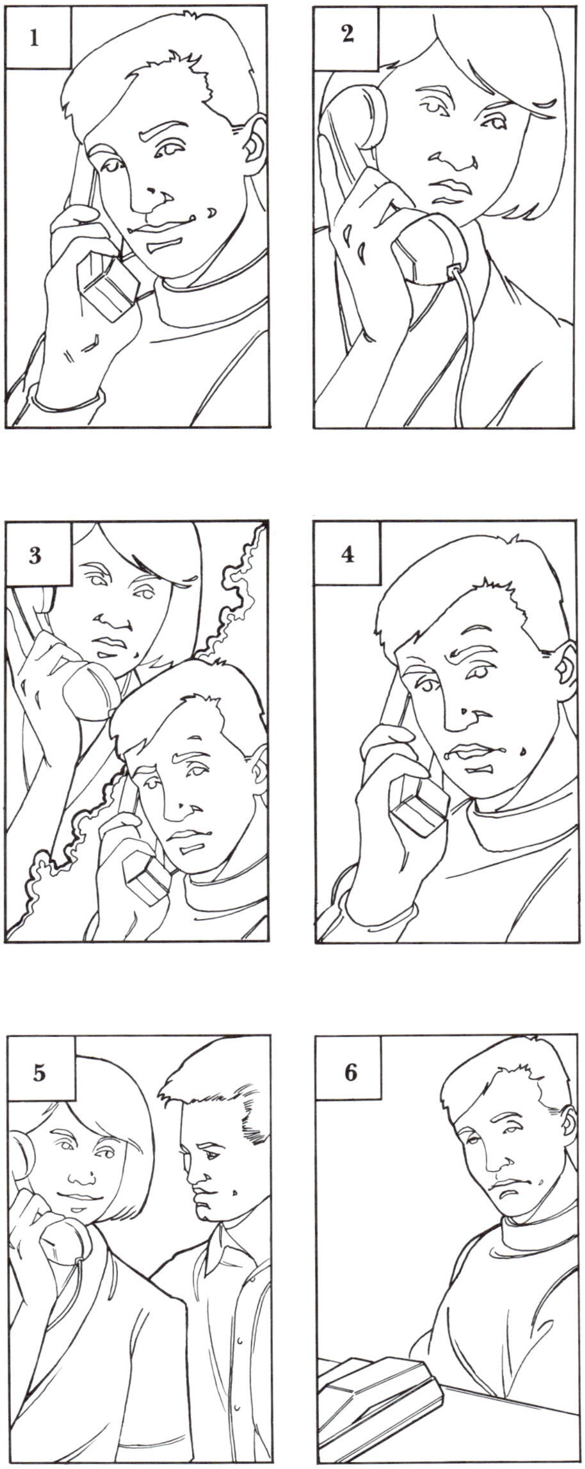

PRACTICE

Where are you going for your holidays?

Look at the example, think of a holiday you would like, and then fill in number 1 with your holiday plans. Then ask three other students about *their* plans, so that you can fill in numbers 2, 3 and 4.

Can you find someone to travel with?

	Name	Country	Transport	Stay
Example	*Paul*	*France*	*by car*	*2 weeks*
1				
2				
3				
4				

In your exercise book, write one of the dialogues that you had with another student.

PART B

START UP

In pairs, talk about:

1 What sort of things do people sometimes invite you to do?
2 Do you always accept invitations?
3 What sort of invitations do you like best?

Function Focus

Inviting, Accepting and Refusing

This is how we use simple expressions of inviting, refusing and accepting.

Inviting

Would you like to + verb
Do you fancy
How about + verb + *ing*
What about

Accepting

Yes, that would be a pleasure.
Yes, please, I'd love to.
Yes, great idea!
Yes, lovely!

Refusing

Well, I'm afraid I'm busy.
Well, I'm afraid I can't + verb + *then.*
Well, I'm afraid I don't like + verb + *ing.*

PRACTICE

These sentences are all part of one dialogue, but they are in the wrong order.

Put the sentences in the right order, and then copy the dialogue in your exercise book.

1 Well, I'm afraid I don't like dancing.
2 Saturday evening? Nothing much.
3 Good idea. I'd love to!
4 What are you doing on Saturday evening?
5 How about coming to the cinema, then?
6 Do you fancy coming to a disco?

PRONUNCIATION

Listen to the tape and practise saying the phrases quickly.

The shortened form of 'do you' sounds like 'joo'.

DEVELOPMENT 1

A Invite your partner to do different things with you. Your partner can accept or refuse.

Here are some ideas:

party disco meal walk meet my mother look at my photos

B Arrange an evening out with your friends. Use your diary to help you.

Student 1 Look at the diary.
Student 2 Turn to page 123.
Student 3 Turn to page 123.
Student 1 This is a page from your diary. You want to arrange an evening out with some other students. You want to go for a meal, and then on to a disco. Find out when the other students are free.

Saturday	*going to the disco*
Sunday	*visiting my friend in hospital,*
	7.00 – 8.00p.m.
Monday	*all-day conference, then dinner*
Tuesday	
Wednesday	
Thursday	
Friday	*theatre*

You might have conversations like this:

Speaker 1 *What are you doing on Thursday evening, Richard?*
Speaker 2 *I'm going to the theatre with my cousin on Thursday.*
Speaker 1 *Oh, well what are you doing on Sunday?*

LISTENING

A Listen to the dialogue, and write down the answers to these questions:

1 What did she do at the weekend?
2 Did she like it?
3 Who was in it?

B Now listen again, and tick any of the following words you hear:

1	director	5	photography	9	seat
2	actor	6	subtitle	10	screen
3	actress	7	review	11	box-office
4	sound-track	8	trailer	12	row

VOCABULARY

Here are six definitions of words you did *not* hear in the dialogue. Write the words beside their definitions.

1 A critical article about a film. ______________
2 A man who acts. ______________
3 A woman who acts. ______________
4 A short piece from a film which is coming to the cinema soon. ______________
5 The person who tells people in the film what to do. ______________
6 Translated dialogue on the screen. __________

DEVELOPMENT 2

In groups, each student think of a film that you saw recently.

Using words in the Vocabulary exercise, discuss why you liked or disliked the film.

WRITING

A Are these invitations formal or informal? What do you think? Write in the spaces underneath each invitation the word *formal* or *informal*.

1
Dear Rachel

Please come to my party
At 14 Poplar Lane, Highbury
Date 4th December Time ....
From ....

Dear .... Thanks for the invitation
☐ I would love to come ☐ I am unable to attend
From ....

2
James and Barbara Brown
Request the pleasure of your company
at 8.30 pm
on 16 th April

RSVP
21, St James St.
Ealing
London
Tel 081 863 2549

Dress formal

3
We're having a party on Saturday at 8 o'clock.
Please come, and bring a friend.
Yours, George.

4
Dinner tonight.
Are you doing anything?
— love Sue.

5
JENNY AND MARGARET
ARE HAVING A FANCY DRESS PARTY
ON SATURDAY 15TH JUNE
9.00 ONWARDS
RSVP

B You are having a party, and this is one of the invitations you are sending to your friends. Fill it in as appropriate.

.... IS HAVING A PARTY
ON ....
AT .... O'CLOCK
AT ....
TEL ....
HOPE YOU CAN COME!

VOCABULARY BANK

I often *invite* my friends to a meal.

Are you going to *accept* the *invitation* to John's birthday party?

Of course! I never *refuse* an invitation!

I'm sorry, I can't come tonight. *I'm afraid I'm busy.*

Go to the cinema with you? Yes, please, *I'd love to.*

My favourite *actress* was in the *film* on TV last night. Did you watch it?

No. Flash Harry was in it, and I think he's a terrible *actor.*

UNIT 7

PART A

START UP

In pairs, look at the two photographs and discuss the questions:

1 Which photo was taken in the USA, and which in the UK?
2 How do you know?
3 What are some of the differences between the two countries? Here are some ideas to help you:

the food *the buildings* *the way of life* *cars*
clothes *music* *crime* *TV*

READING

There are a lot of sayings about home: 'Home sweet home', 'There's no place like home', and 'An Englishman's home is his castle.' Some people think their home and their home country are better than others. Take the British and the Americans, for example.

You will read two articles. The first is a magazine article written by a rather critical Englishman called Geoffrey Plum.

A **In pairs, discuss what sort of critical comments you think Mr Plum might make about the USA.**

B **Read his article. Many people do not agree with him. Do you?**

The Americans are very proud of their country. They say that in the USA the buildings are taller, the cigars are longer, the cars are bigger, and the girls are prettier than anywhere in the world.
The English don't always agree. Some say the Americans are louder, richer and noisier than any other nationality. Other British people think there are lots of good things about the USA like Hollywood, jazz and Superman. It is true that most American skyscrapers are taller than buildings in the UK, but I think that our stately homes are older and more beautiful than anything in the USA.
The Americans love coke and hamburgers – people in the UK think British food is much healthier. Clothes are cheaper in the US but fashion design in the UK is better than design in the USA.
And the women ...? Well, American women certainly are very beautiful; they are taller and slimmer than British women, but I think they know less about the world.
The British prefer their way of life, which is much slower, and their politics, which they think are more sensible. They think a British accent is much better than an American one. The British also think that they are more polite than their American cousins...!

Come to the USA!

America! Land of the free! Land of variety, of big smiles and friendly faces, of endless miles and open spaces! One day the beautiful Grand Canyon, the next the excitement and colour of Las Vegas. Each city is more interesting than the last.
There's so much to see and do. The culture of the Red Indians, the fantastic new architecture, the sound of jazz, the wonders of Disneyland, the delicious taste of barbecued steaks and Baskin Robbins ice-cream... Once you visit America, you go there again and again. The country has magic. The people welcome you, the countryside amazes you, the variety of the food and drink surprises you. If you want a really special holiday, America is friendlier and more exciting than any other country!

C Now read the first article again, and mark these statements true (T) or false (F).

According to the writer of this article, some British people think:

		T	F
1	British women are taller than American women.		
2	British food is healthier than American food.		
3	Clothes are more expensive in the United States.		
4	American women are more educated than British women.		
5	Life is faster in America.		
6	An English accent is better than an American one.		
7	British people make more noise than American people.		

D Read the second article. Underline five adjectives and write down their comparative forms.

Grammar Guide

Making Comparative Adjectives

1 Most adjectives of one or two syllables change their ending, like this:

adjective + *er*	*y* + *ier*	+ *r*	+ last letter,+ *er*	
(1) *funny*	✓			*funnier*
(2) *large*		✓		*larger*
(3) *big*			✓	*bigger*
(4) *great* ✓				*greater*

a *funny* Two-syllable adjectives ending in *-y*: drop the *y* and add *-ier*.

b *large* Adjectives ending in *-e* just add *-r*.

c *big* One-syllable adjectives ending in /consonant – vowel – consonant/, and if the last consonant is *b, d, g, m, n, p*, or *t* double the last letter and add *-er*.

d *great* Other adjectives of one or two syllables: just add *-er*.

(There are exceptions to these rules.)

2 Adjectives with three or more syllables (and some with two syllables!) take *more* before the adjective.
Example:
more beautiful *more careful*

3 Some adjectives have irregular forms:
good *better*
well *better*
bad *worse*

VOCABULARY

Look at this list of comparative adjectives. In pairs, discuss which comparative adjectives have the opposite meaning and write them down.

Example:
The opposite of *richer* is *poorer*.

1 bigger __________
2 smaller __________
3 prettier __________
4 slimmer __________
5 slower __________
6 better __________
7 cheaper (be careful!) __________
8 longer __________

PRACTICE

Many British people love the UK, but they often buy foreign cars. Some think Italian cars are a little faster, others think German cars are far more comfortable.
In the last sentence we made the meaning more exact by using the modifiers *a little* and *far*.

Look at this box:

a little	+ comparative adjective: *it's **a little** bigger than..*
a lot	+ *more/less* + adjective: *it's **a lot** more/less comfortable than...*
far	+ comparative adjective: *it's **far** bigger than...*
much	+ *more/less* + adjective: *it's **much** more/less comfortable than...*

This chart has details about cars from different countries.

In pairs, ask questions such as: *How does the BMW compare with the Alfa?*

Reply using sentences like these:

1 The BMW is a little wider than the Alfa.
2 The Mercedes is a lot faster than the Citroën.
3 The Mini is much cheaper than the BMW.
4 The Mercedes is far more expensive than the Mini.

	Length (m)	Width (m)	Top Speed (mph)	Cost £££
Alfa 33	4.02	1.62	102	10,599
BMW - 3	4.33	1.65	104	16,445
Citroen 2CV	3.83	1.48	66	3,962
Mercedes Benz 190	4.42	1.68	119	27,300
Austin Mini 1275	3.05	1.41	87	4,896

WRITING

How does your home country compare with other countries and the home countries of other students in the class?

Write these headings in your notebooks:

Food *Weather* *The People* *Buildings*
Clothes *The Way of Life*

In pairs, discuss the differences, and make notes under the appropriate headings.

Example:
Weather: warmer and drier.
Food: more interesting and healthier.

PART B

START UP

1

2

3

Each of these photos shows a different national stereotype.

In pairs, decide what nationality the different people are.

1 What helped you decide?
2 Do you agree with these national stereotypes? Why? Why not?

PRONUNCIATION

The names of countries are different from the names of nationalities. Both the word and the stress may be different.

Here is a list of some countries. The little boxes show which syllable is stressed.

A **You will hear the names of some nationalities. Write them down as you hear them.**

B **Listen to the cassette again. This time put a mark above the part of the word which is stressed.**

The first one has been done for you.

1 China ...Chinese
2 Britain
3 Italy
4 Spain
5 Thailand
6 Greece
7 Japan
8 Germany
9 France
10 Turkey
11 Switzerland
12 Iran
13 The Netherlands
14 Malaysia
15 Portugal

Function Focus

Agreeing and Disagreeing

We use these sentences when we agree or disagree with someone:

Agree	Disagree
I agree.	I don't agree.
You're right.	I don't think so.
Yes, I think so too.	That's nonsense!
That's true.	That's not true.

LISTENING

A **On the cassette you will hear two friends at home talking about people of different nationalities. They do not agree! Listen to them and look at the Function Focus. Put a tick beside the sentences you hear.**

B **Listen to the cassette again. Listen to what the speakers say and fill in the chart below with adjectives and comparative adjectives.**

Nationality	What the speakers say
British	
American	
Italian	
Japanese	
Swiss	
Spanish	

DEVELOPMENT

Which of these adjectives do you think describe the different nationalities?

Write the appropriate adjective/adjectives beside the nationalities. Compare your results with your partner. Do you agree or disagree?

serious *friendly* *hard-working* *happy*
sophisticated *excitable* *noisy* *unsophisticated*
fun-loving *unfriendly* *warm* *quiet* *lazy*

Nationality	Description
1 British	
2 French	
3 Italian	
4 Spanish	
5 Swiss	
6 German	
7 Japanese	
8 American	
9 Brazilian	
10 Mexican	

VOCABULARY BANK

Most people are proud of their *homes* and their *home countries.*
This dress is *prettier* and *cheaper* than that one.
People in the cities are sometimes *unfriendly.*
People in the country are usually *friendly.*
The Japanese are very *hard-working*; they are never *lazy.*
Parisian women are often very *sophisticated.*
Americans are sometimes rather *noisy.*

UNIT 8

PART A

START UP

In pairs, discuss:

1 What is happening in the picture?
2 What is the name of the shop in the picture?
3 Do you like this kind of shop? Why? Why not?
4 Do you shop in the Sales?

LISTENING

A You will hear a radio programme about shopping. It gives details about Harrods.

As you listen, answer the questions.

1 Most people agree that Harrods is:
   a the most expensive store in London.
   b the best store in London.
   c the worst store in London.
2 It is the:
   a largest and most famous shop in the UK.
   b largest and most famous shop in the world.
   c largest and most crowded shop in London.
3 The biggest cash sale was:
   a two million two hundred thousand pounds.
   b two hundred thousand pounds.
   c two million pounds.
4 The shop's busiest times are:
   a June and July.
   b Christmas and the Sales.
   c Christmas and New Year.
5 The first day of the Sales is:
   a the most crowded.
   b the easiest.
   c the quietest.
6 One of the most popular buys at Christmas is:
   a Christmas cake.
   b Christmas cards.
   c Christmas pudding.
7 One of the most unusual exports was:
   a sixty Rolls-Royces to New York.
   b six bread rolls to New York.
   c half a kilogram of sausages to New York.

B Listen to the cassette again and answer the following questions:

1 What famous people shop in Harrods?
2 How many people shop in Harrods every day?
3 How many people go into Harrods on the first day of the Sales?
4 How many Christmas puddings do they sell every year?
5 What other unusual exports do you hear about?

Grammar Guide

Superlatives

In Unit 7 you learned the rules about how to make comparative adjectives.

Example:

*American buildings are **newer than** British ones.*
*American women are **taller than** British women.*

Comparative usually means comparing TWO different things. When we want to compare one thing with two or more other things we can use the superlative form:
The superlative form looks like this:
'Building B is the biggest, and building D is the smallest.'

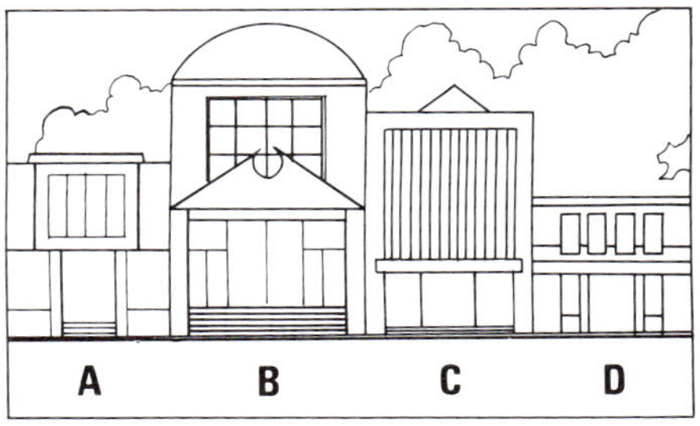

We often need to say more than this.

Example:

The CN Tower in Toronto is the highest tower in the world.
The IBA Tower at Emley Moor is the highest tower in the UK.

Superlatives are formed like this:

Adjective	Comparative	Superlative
funny	*funnier*	*the funniest*
large	*larger*	*the largest*
big	*bigger*	*the biggest*
great	*greater*	*the greatest*

Superlatives also take *the most* and *the least* in the same way that comparatives take *more* and *less*.

Example:

***the most** difficult*
***the least** interesting*

Learn the few exceptions:

Adjective	Comparative	Superlative
good	*better*	*the best*
bad	*worse*	*the worst*
little	*less*	*the least*
many	*more*	*the most*

PRACTICE

A When you go shopping you sometimes hear sentences like these.

Compare them, using the superlative. Remember to use *the most* and *the least* as appropriate.

The first has been done for you.

1. It's ...(cheap)... thing in the shop.
   It's *the cheapest* thing in the shop.
2. Is that ...(large)... size you've got?
3. You can get ...(good)... bargains in the Sales.
4. This is ...(tiny)... watch I can find.
5. You shouldn't buy anything there. It's ...(bad)... shop in this town.
6. Is that ...(fat)... chicken you can offer me?
7. I don't like it. It's ...(attractive)... present in the store. (careful!)
8. They're ...(expensive)... ones you can buy.

B The Jones are going to tour Switzerland, Italy, and Spain. Mrs Jones loves shopping. These are the pages she tore from some travel guides. What are the best things to buy in the three countries they are visiting?

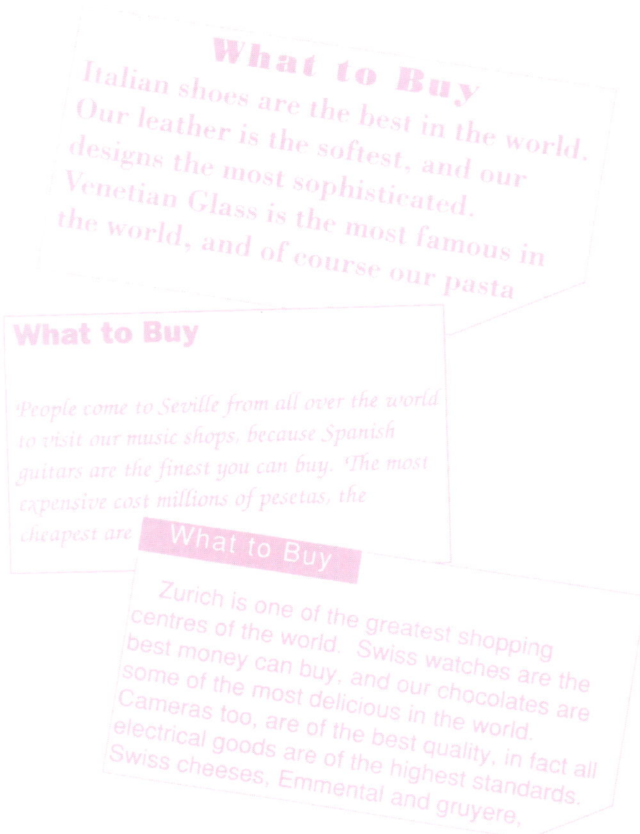
What to Buy
Italian shoes are the best in the world. Our leather is the softest, and our designs the most sophisticated. Venetian Glass is the most famous in the world, and of course our pasta

What to Buy
People come to Seville from all over the world to visit our music shops, because Spanish guitars are the finest you can buy. The most expensive cost millions of pesetas, the cheapest are

What to Buy
Zurich is one of the greatest shopping centres of the world. Swiss watches are the best money can buy, and our chocolates are some of the most delicious in the world. Cameras too, are of the best quality, in fact all electrical goods are of the highest standards. Swiss cheeses, Emmental and gruyere.

C **Tell your partner what you think are the best goods to buy from any countries you have visited or in your own country.**

D **In pairs, look at this list of goods and the countries they come from.**

Goods	**Countries producing them**		
Clothes	France	Italy	Spain
Watches	Switzerland	Japan	America
Wine	France	Portugal	Greece
Guitars	Spain	Japan	Portugal
Chocolates	England	Switzerland	France
Carpets	Turkey	Iran	Morocco
Pearls	The Middle East	Japan	China
Silk	Thailand	China	India
Cars	Italy	England	Germany

Discuss and decide which countries you think produce the best. Remember to use ways of agreeing and disagreeing that you learnt in the last unit.

Example:

Speaker 1 *I think Kenyan coffee is better than Colombian or Turkish coffee.*

Speaker 2 *I don't agree, I think Colombian coffee is the best.*

When you decide which country produces the best, underline it.

Remember: clothes from France are French clothes, clothes from Italy are Italian.

START UP

PART B

In this shop window you can see some winter clothes.

Fill in the spaces in the shop window as appropriate with these words:

a pair of gloves   *a skirt*   *a scarf*   *a jacket*
a pair of trousers   *a coat*   *a jumper*
a cardigan   *a pair of boots*   *a shirt*

Function Focus

Conversations for Shopping

Read these dialogues, and practise them in pairs.

Buying It or Leaving It

When we go to a shop to buy clothes, we may have a conversation like this:

A Can I help you?

B Yes please. Can I try this on? / these on? — B No thanks, I'm just looking.

A Certainly... How is it? / are they?

B It's / They're fine. I'll take it. / them. — B I think I'll leave it / them thanks.

Speaker 1	Can I help you?
Speaker 2	Yes please. Can I try this on?/these on?
Speaker 2	No thanks, I'm just looking.
Speaker 1	Certainly...How is it?/are they?
Speaker 2	It's/They're fine. I'll take it/them.
Speaker 2	I think I'll leave it/them thanks.

The Size and the Price

We may have conversations like these about the size and the price of things:

A How much is this coat? / are these trousers? → B It's £105.00 / They're £25.00

A What size is it? / are they? → B It's / They're small/medium/large.

A Can I try it on? / them on? → B Sure.

A It's / They're too big/small. Have you got a smaller / bigger size?

Speaker 1	How much is this coat?/are these trousers?
Speaker 2	It's £105.00./They're £25.00.
Speaker 1	What size is it?/are they?
Speaker 2	It's/They're small/medium/large.
Speaker 1	Can I try it on?/them on?
Speaker 2	Sure.
Speaker 1	It's/They're too big /small. Have you got a smaller/bigger size?

PRACTICE

Work in pairs.

Student 1 You are a shopper.
Student 2 You are the shop assistant.

Student 1 Look at the illustration on page 32.
Student 2 Look at the list on page 123 of the Appendices.

Student 1 You are at the Sales and you have £40.00 to spend. You want to buy two things. Decide your size — are you small, medium or large? Ask Student 2 about the prices and the sizes of the clothes. Leave the clothes if they are the wrong size or too expensive. Buy the clothes if they are the right size and the right price. When you have bought your two things, change roles with your partner.

LISTENING

Listen to the following dialogues about shopping and fill in the chart.

Item	Cost	Size	Does the customer buy it/them?
a			
b			
c			
d			

PRONUNCIATION

Can you say the price correctly?

If the price is less than a pound: always pronounce the *p*, for example, 47**p**, 94**p.**

If the price is more than a pound: don't pronounce the *p*, for example, **£**1.50, **£**24.49

SELF-HELP

You have seen some of these instructions. Match them to the items a–f.

a	b	c	d	e	f
~~word~~	✓	(word)	<u>word</u>	[word]	✗

1 Put a tick.
2 Put a cross.
3 Underline.
4 Put a box round.
5 Put a circle round.
6 Cross out.

VOCABULARY BANK

The *best* day to go to the *Sales* is the first day.

The *cheapest* things go first; the *most expensive* are still in the shops at the end of the Sales!

The *price* of *clothes* has gone up so much – they *cost* much less a few years ago.

Is your *size small, medium* or *large*?

UNIT 9

PART A

START UP

Look at the picture.

1 What's the girl's job?

2 Do you think it's an interesting job?

3 What's your ideal job? Why?

Grammar Guide

The Present Perfect Tense

We form the present perfect with the present tense of have and the past participle of the main verb.

Affirmative	*You have*	*worked...*
	He/she has	
Negative	*You haven't*	*worked...*
	He/she hasn't	
Interrogative	*Have you*	*worked?*
	Has he/she	
Short answers	*Yes I have.*	
	Yes he/she has.	
	No I haven't.	
	No he/she hasn't.	

Remember to be careful of irregular verbs. For a list of common irregular verbs see the Appendices, page 122.

We use the present perfect very often:

1 To talk about something which began in the past but has a link with the present.
Example:
I've lived here all my life.
Link: *I'm still living here.*

2 To talk about our experiences.
Example:
I have been to America.
Link: *It's part of my experiences.*

3 To talk about events.
Example:
The meeting has begun.
Link: *It is still taking place.*

The Present Perfect Tense Adverbs

We can use these adverbs with the present perfect:
Just is used in interrogative and affirmative sentences.
Example:
Mr Jones has just left.
(This means that Mr Jones left the office only one or two minutes ago.)

Yet is only used in interrogative and negative sentences.
Example:
Has Mr Bond arrived yet?
No, he hasn't (arrived yet).

For is used with a period of time.
Example:
She has lived here for three years.

Since is used with a point in time.
Example:
She has lived here since 1989.

VOCABULARY 1

Do the words in this list refer to points of time or periods of time?

Put them in the correct column!

last week *seven days* *May, 1965*
a few minutes *an hour* *Thursday*
a fortnight *midnight* *the last fifty years*
the beginning of June

For **(periods of time)**	***Since*** **(points of time)**

PRACTICE 1

In pairs ask and answer questions using the present perfect with *for* and *since*.

Start like this:

Speaker 1 Where do you live?
Speaker 2 I live in __________ .
Speaker 1 How long have you lived there?
Speaker 2 I've lived there for __________ / since __________ .

Now use these verbs to ask and answer more questions:

study English *work* *study at this school*
know your partner

Now think of some other questions for your partner to answer.

LISTENING

A **Look at the picture at the top of page 34. This woman has started her own business recently.**

1 What kind of business has she started?
2 What kind of problems might she have in her work?

B A journalist is visiting local businesses. He is interviewing people who have started their own businesses. He wants to write an article about them for the local paper.

Listen to the three business people talk about their businesses, the difficulties they have met, and the successes they have had. Mark these sentences true (T) or false (F):

		T	F
1	Running her own fashion business has been easy for Tracy.		
2	She has often thought about giving it up.		
3	Some people haven't paid for the clothes she made for them.		
4	Peter has started his own language school.		
5	Starting his own business has been very exciting for him.		
6	He has had a lot of experience in marketing.		
7	He hasn't done much advertising.		
8	Ken has set up as a telephone hygienist.		
9	He has had a lot of calls about business.		
10	He says he has been very lucky.		

C **Listen to the cassette again, and fill in the chart as you listen:**

Name	**Length of time in business**	**Have they had problems?**	**Has the business been a success?**
Fashion designer			
School director			
Telephone hygienist			

D **Listen to the cassette again.**

What have Tracy, Peter and Ken just done?

Remember to put *just* between the auxiliary and the verb.

Example:
*She has **just** finished a dress.*

1 Tracy __________________________
2 Peter __________________________
3 Ken __________________________

PRACTICE 2

With your partner, talk about different things that you or your family have done recently.

Example:

*I've **just** passed an exam.*
*My father has **just** bought a new car.*
*We have **just** moved house.*

VOCABULARY 2

The words in the first column were on the cassette. The words in the second column have the opposite meaning.

They are jumbled. Match them!
The first has been done for you.

1 loss (g)	**a** to close down
2 to set up	**b** to make redundant
3 a success	**c** employee
4 to borrow	**d** a failure
5 to sell	**e** to lend
6 employer	**f** to buy
7 to employ	**g** profit

PRONUNCIATION

Listen to the cassette and practise the pronunciation of the contractions in these sentences.

1 He's had a rise.
2 We've made a new plan.
3 I've been away on business.
4 They've sold the company.
5 You've decided to move.
6 The company's been very successful.

PRACTICE 3

Tracy is very busy because she's having a fashion show soon. She has worked all morning, and it's now one o'clock, but she hasn't done everything yet. This is the list of things to do which she has made. Some things are crossed off because she has just done them, but there are some things she hasn't done yet.

Work in pairs.

Student 1 Ask a question.
Student 2 Reply.

Example:

Has she booked the room for the show?
No, she hasn't booked it yet.
Has she sent the invitations?
Yes, she's just sent them.

PART B

START UP

Tracy is talking to a small business consultant.
The consultant is making suggestions to help Tracy with her problems.
What do you think the consultant is saying?

> Starting your own business? Get it right.
> Those first early steps taken are
> the future success of your business.
> Take those steps in the right direction - contact us!
> MORTON ASSOCIATES. Tel: 081 499 0321

Function Focus

f

Suggestions and Responses

In Column A there are ways of making suggestions.
In Column B there are ways of responding.

Column A		Column B
Why don't you... *You could*	*+ verb stem*	*That's a good idea!* *Why haven't I thought of that?*
Try *What about...*	*verb + -ing*	*Well, I don't think that's a good idea, really.* *Brilliant!*

Look at these examples of the consultant's suggestions:

1 Why don't you borrow some money?
2 You could move to a bigger workshop.
3 Try employing more people to help you.

Note the use of the *-ing* form after the verb *to try*, and the phrase *what about*.

DEVELOPMENT

Student 1 You are the consultant and Tracy is asking you for advice. Read the advice sheet below. Tracy will explain her problems to you. Use the information on the advice sheet and your own ideas to make suggestions. Use the phrases you have learnt in the Function Focus.

Student 2 Turn to page 123 of the Appendices. Your instructions are there.

Advice Sheet for small businesses

Problems	Possible solutions
Not enough money	borrow some/sell your house/get a rich partner.
Not enough workers	employ strangers–never ask your family or friends to work for you
Sales are bad	Advertise more/look at the competition
The advertising doesn't work	Advertising must be very frequent to be successful
Some workers are difficult	Dismiss them-fast and kindly
Tax forms are impossible	Get an accountant to do them
There's never any money in the bank	Don't write any cheques until you have to

PRACTICE

In Column A is a list of some problems small businesses have. In Column B is a list of suggested solutions – but they do not match.

Work in pairs, Student 1 and Student 2 each read a column.

Student 1 Read out the first problem.
Student 2 Look through the possible suggestions, and read out the best one.
Student 1 Respond. Use one of the phrases in the Function Focus.

Column A	Column B
1 I need more money.	a What about advertising to increase your sales?
2 I need more staff.	b Why don't you get an accountant?
3 I don't understand tax.	c Try borrowing from the bank.
4 I can't sell enough.	d You could employ school leavers; they're cheap.
5 I've got too much work.	e Why don't you get a partner to help you?

WRITING

Work in pairs.

Choose a business that interests you both, and write notes about:

1 how much money you must have to start your business.
2 how many people you will employ.
3 where you are going to start your business.
4 how you will advertise.
5 who will buy your goods/services.
6 how much money you must borrow from the bank.
7 how soon you can re-pay the money.

Think of as many good ideas about this business as you can, and don't forget to make suggestions to your partner!

Make a spoken presentation of your ideas to the rest of the class.

VOCABULARY BANK

Put the words into sentences and copy them into your vocabulary books.

started up *success* *problems* *borrowed*
employed *advice* *suggestions* *fail*

UNIT 10

PART A

START UP

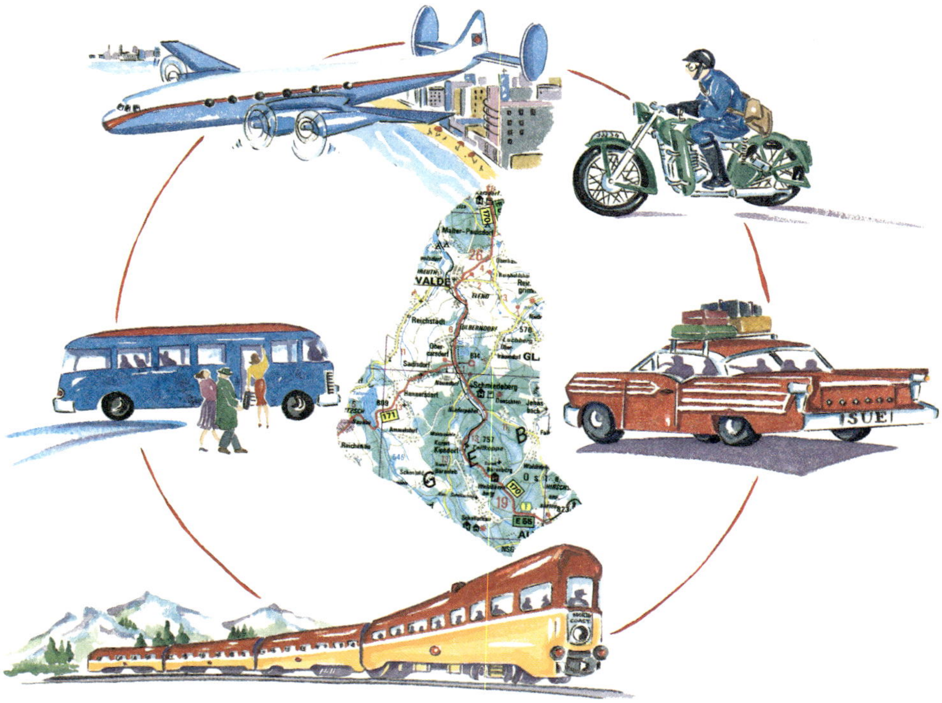

Look at this picture.

It shows people travelling in different ways.

What are these ways?

People choose many different ways to travel.

Talk to your partner about the different ways in which you have travelled.

Make three or four comparative sentences about each part of the picture.

Example:
Flying is the most expensive way of travelling.
Trains are the most comfortable.
Cars are quicker than coaches.
Coaches are cheaper than trains.

1 What are the best and worst ways of travelling, and why?
2 What are the best and worst trips you have had?

LISTENING

A travel writer is collecting stories for a book called *This Is The Worst Trip I've Ever Been On.* She is talking to a traveller about a bad trip.

Look at the questions and listen to the story, told by Lucy. Write down the answers to the questions as you listen.

1 Has Lucy always enjoyed travelling?
2 In which place did she have the most frightening experience of her life?
3 Was she alone?
4 What did she do when she saw the man's arm?
5 Has she been back to Los Pulcres?

WRITING

Now write four headings in your notebooks:

Where *When* *Who with* *What happened?*

Now listen to the story, more than once if necessary, and take notes. Write your notes under the appropriate heading. You do not need to write complete sentences. Write down at least one piece of information under each heading, and if you can, write more.

DEVELOPMENT

In groups, discuss other stories you have heard of travellers who had unpleasant experiences.

PRACTICE

A **Look at the photos of these famous places. In which cities are they?**

In pairs, Student 1 and Student 2, have conversations like this:

Student 1 *I've seen Buckingham Palace.*
Student 2 *Oh, so you've been to London?*
Student 1 *That's right, I have.*

When you have finished talking about the photos, continue using your own ideas.

Ask questions like this:

Student 1 *Have you seen the Prado?*
Student 2 *Yes, I have.*
No, I've never been to Madrid.

B Tom wants to go round the world and is looking for someone to travel with. He has met Terry. They are deciding where to go. Tom is suggesting different places, but Terry has already been to many of them.

Before you do this exercise, look at the Function Focus of Unit 9 to revise suggestions and responses.

Tom What about going to India?
Terry Well, I don't think that's a good idea. I've already been there.
Tom We could visit Australia.
Terry I've already been there, too.
Tom Have you been to Thailand yet?
Terry Um, yes, I have. Sorry!
Tom Well, have you got any suggestions?
Terry Try finding somebody else to go with!

Now cover the dialogue. In pairs, Student 1 and Student 2, practise it.

Student 1	**Student 2**
India?	response
Australia?	response
Thailand?	response
suggestions?	go on your own
response	

Now change roles.

C **The two of you are going round the world, but you have only two months. You will start in Japan, and carry all your luggage in a rucksack. Discuss which countries to visit, and how long to stay there, and what you must take on your trip.**

Make a note of your plans using this list.

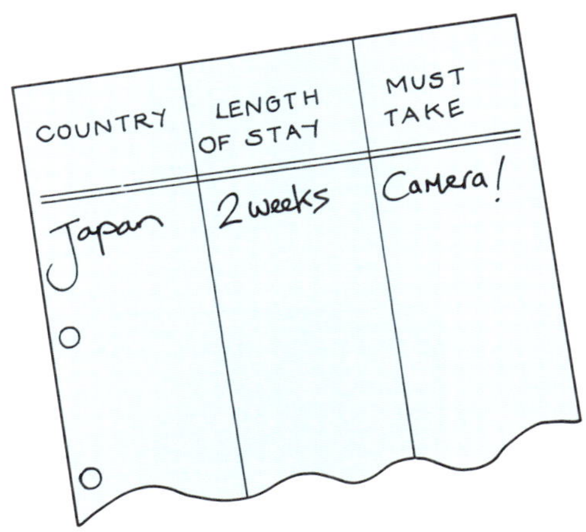

START UP

PART B

In pairs, look at the photographs and write a sentence about each one, using a superlative.

PRACTICE

Are these statements true or false?

Discuss them in pairs and put a tick in the right column. Don't forget to use the language of agreement and disagreement.

Example:

Student 1 *Well, I think the Amazon is longer than the Nile.*

Student 2 *I don't agree, I think the Nile is longer.*

Before you begin, look at the Function Focus of Unit 7, and check ways of agreeing and disagreeing.

	T	F
1 The most expensive painting sold in the 1980s was by Picasso.		
2 Concorde is the fastest airliner in the world.		
3 The Nile is longer than the Amazon.		
4 The Atlantic Ocean is bigger than the Pacific Ocean.		
5 The most widely-spoken language in the world is Mandarin Chinese.		
6 The highest waterfall in the world is in Venezuela.		
7 The longest word in the world is in the German language.		

VOCABULARY

What are the opposites of the words below?

The first has been done for you.

1 safe / *dangerous*

2 comfortable __________

3 sophisticated __________

4 difficult __________

5 careful __________

6 loudest __________

7 useless __________

8 worst __________

9 worse __________

DEVELOPMENT

A Make two teams.

Each team chooses a secretary.

In your teams, think of ten questions such as: *'What is the fastest animal in the world?'* or *'What is the highest mountain in Scotland?'*

You must know the answers.

The Secretary writes down the ten questions and the answers, and gives them to the teacher, who acts as quiz-master.

B In small groups, talk about your own travels, in your own country as well as abroad.

1 Did you have any problems, difficulties or dangers?

2 Do you like travelling on your own? Why? Why not?

3 Is it more difficult for a woman to travel on her own than a man?

4 How did you overcome any language problems on your travels?

5 What advice do you have for travellers visiting (a) the UK, (b) your own country?

VOCABULARY BANK

Flying is the *fastest* way to *travel.*

I'm *going on a trip* round the world!

Travellers sometimes have *frightening* or *unpleasant experiences.*

Remember your passport when you are *travelling*!

START UP

Look at the pictures.

They show two young women in a job interview. The woman on the bottom is called Mary. The woman on the top is Linda. Mary did not get the job, although she has more experience than Linda.

In pairs, discuss:

1 What is Mary doing wrong? (At least three things.)
2 What is Linda doing right? (At least three things.)

Grammar Guide

The Past Simple and Present Perfect Tenses

The past simple tense is used for finished action or experience.
I was a taxi driver (after I left school).
I studied law (from 1987 to 1990).
I worked in a bank (for five years).

The present perfect tense is used to link past action or experience with present time.
I have lived in this town all my life (I'm still living in it.)
I have worked here for twelve years. (I'm still working here.)

VOCABULARY

Linda is telling a friend about her interview.

Look at this list of words, and use them to fill the gaps.

experience *interview* *details* *apply*
interviewers *candidate* *present* *skills*

Well, I saw the job in the paper and decided to (1) ________ immediately. I was called for an (2) ________ the next week. When I got there, there was one other (3) ________ waiting. I went in first. The (4) ________ were quite nice, a man and a woman. They asked me about my (5) ________ job. Then they asked me about my (6) ________ and I said I worked in a hotel during my school holidays. They asked me about my secretarial (7) ________ too, and I said I had typing and word processing. They wanted (8) ________ about any previous illnesses and then they said: 'When can you start?'

PRACTICE 1

Which of the time phrases below is used with the past simple, and which with the present perfect?

Write sentences about your own life using the time phrases, and put them under the appropriate headings.

at Christmas just on Saturday since 1980
yesterday for a long time last year already
3 minutes ago yet at 6 o'clock for 5 hours

Past simple **Present perfect**

Ever/never

Look at these questions and answers:

*Have you **ever** worked in an office?* *Yes I have.*
*Has he **ever** driven a taxi?* *No, he hasn't.*
*No, **never**.*

Ever means in the person's life (up to the present time).
We usually use *ever* in questions and *never* in negative statements.

PRACTICE 2

In pairs, look at these pictures.

They show places where people work.
What are they? For example, Picture 1 is a hotel.

Now use these prompts to find out about your partner's work experience. Make dialogues about each picture, such as:

Dialogue A
Have you ever worked in a hotel?
Yes, I have.
When did you work there?
Three years ago/last year/in the summer.
What did you do?
I was a waiter/waitress.

Dialogue B
Have you ever worked in a hotel?
No, never. Have you?
Yes, I have.
What did you do?
I was a waiter/waitress.

Make similar dialogues about an office, a factory, a restaurant and a school.

Your final question can be: *Where else have you worked?*

DEVELOPMENT

In groups of three, ask each other these questions:

1 Have you ever been for an interview?
2 What job was it for?
3 What questions did they ask?
4 How long was the interview?
5 What questions do interviewers usually ask their candidates?
6 What do candidates usually have to do before they get an interview?

LISTENING

Linda is having an interview. The people interviewing her are making notes as she answers their questions.

A Look at the form below. Then listen to the interview, and fill in the form.

Fitz Hotel Personnel Recruitment Form

Part A
Name: Miss Simpson
Interviewed by: Pat White and
Telephone: 081 365 8362
Job applied for:
Skills:
Experience:
Present job:

Part B
1 School
2 Exams
3 Languages
4 Length of time in present job
5 Reason for leaving
6 Present salary
7 Experience in hotel work Yes No
Details
8 Dismissals Yes No

B Now look at the form again.

What questions did the interviewer ask to fill in Part B of the form?

The first question has been done for you.

1 *Which school did you go to?*
2 What_______________________________?
3 What_______________________________?
4 How long_______________________________?
5 Why_______________________________?
6 What_______________________________?
7 Have_______________________________?
When_______________________________?
8 Have_______________________________?

C Listen to the cassette again and compare your questions to those on the cassette.

PART B

START UP

In pairs, look at the cartoon, and discuss these questions:

1 Do you think most interviewers are like the ones in the cartoon?
2 How do you usually feel in interviews, confident or nervous? Why?
3 Talk about the worst interview you have had.

LISTENING

You will hear four short dialogues from a TV interview. In each dialogue one of the speakers uses one of the phrases in the Function Focus below to check meaning.

Listen to the dialogues, and put a tick beside all the phrases you hear.

PRONUNCIATION

Now you will hear the phrases on cassette. Listen carefully to the intonation, and repeat them.

Function Focus

Checking Meanings

We often need to check things when we are listening to someone:

1 When we haven't heard:
I'm sorry?
I'm sorry, could you repeat that please?
What did you say?

2 When we want to understand something more clearly:
What does ... mean?
What exactly do you mean?

3 When we want to check a fact:
When exactly was that?
What exactly did you do?
How do you spell that?

DEVELOPMENT

In pairs, Student 1 and Student 2, interview each other for the job of chef at the Fitz Hotel.

Student 1 You are the interviewer. Do not look at the CV on this page. Look at the form on page 123 of the Appendices. Complete the form by asking your partner questions such as:

Have you ever...?
When did you...?

Don't forget to check meanings and ask any other questions that you think are necessary.

Student 2 You are the candidate. Look at your CV. Use it to answer your partner's questions. Some of the information you need is missing. Use your imagination! Don't forget to check meanings of questions using the phrases you have learnt. Do not look at the form your partner is filling in.

When you have finished, change roles.

CV

Name:	(your name)
Age:	(your age)
Address:	(your address)
Telephone:	(your telephone number)
Experience:	Kitchen work during military service, (18 months). Cooking for friends' wedding parties. Kitchen assistant at Berni Inn (1 year). Assistant Meat Chef at the Intercontinental Hotel (2 years). Chef in my own restaurant (3 years) (present job).
Skills:	Meat dishes, organising large parties,running a restaurant, accounts, management.
Education:	Saint Mary's High School. Castle Hill Technical College, Diploma in Cooking.
Languages:	French.

VOCABULARY BANK

From this point on the Vocabulary Banks will be in the form of word lists, not complete sentences.

Put the words into sentences and copy them into your vocabulary books

application *details* *experience* *interview*
interviewer *job* *skills* *to apply* *to check*
to spell

UNIT 12

PART A

START UP

The picture shows a typical scene in a modern British home.

A How are household jobs divided in your home?

In pairs, talk about the jobs listed in the grid, and tick the appropriate boxes.

Job	For Men	For Women	For Both
Cooking			
Cleaning			
Car washing			
Gardening			
Child care			
Paying the bills			
Shopping			
Repairing the car			
Painting the house			
Sewing			
Washing the dishes			
Drying the dishes			

B **Change partners. Compare your answers.**

Do you agree with the way jobs are divided in the house?

Grammar Guide

Quite a Lot* and *Not Much/Many

Look at this table:

How much/How many + Noun + Verb?

Examples:

1 *How much cooking do you do?* (Cooking is not countable.)
Quite a lot / Not much.

2 *How many dishes can you cook?* (Dishes are countable.)
Quite a lot / Not many.

How much (not countable)	How many (countable)
a lot	*a lot*
quite a lot	*quite a lot/quite a few*
not much	*not many*
a little	*only a few*
only a little	*hardly any*
none	*none*

PRACTICE 1

In pairs, look at the picture.

Discuss the questions and tick the correct answer.

1 How many dirty dishes are there?
- **a** not much
- **b** a lot
- **c** not many

2 How much bread is there?
- **a** hardly any
- **b** only a few
- **c** quite a lot

3 How many cups are there?
- **a** quite a few
- **b** not much
- **c** not many

4 How much milk is there?
- **a** only a little
- **b** only a few
- **c** none

5 How many clean dishes are there?
- **a** not many
- **b** not much
- **c** quite a lot

READING

A How liberated are you? Find out with this questionnaire from a magazine.

Questionnaire A is for men.

Questionnaire B is for women.

Read the questions and tick the appropriate spaces in the chart.

		a lot	quite a lot	not much	a little	only a little	none	quite a lot/ quite a few	not many	only a few	hardly any
A	**For the men**										
1	How much washing-up do you do a week?										
2	How much shopping do you do?										
3	How many nights a week do you cook?										
4	How much experience do you have of babies?										
5	How many different dishes can you cook?										
6	How much sewing do you do?										
7	How much time do you spend cleaning the house every week?										
B	**For the women**										
1	How much experience do you have of repairing cars?										
2	How many bouquets have you bought for a man?										
3	How many times have you invited your man out to dinner?										
4	How much do you know about fixing things in the house?										
5	How many times have you driven a car too fast?										
6	Do/did you want to get married? How much?										
7	How many times have you been on holiday on your own?										

B In pairs, compare your charts.

How liberated do you think your partner is?

- **a** very liberated
- **b** quite liberated
- **c** not very liberated
- **d** not liberated at all

Explain your decision to your partner!

PRACTICE 2

In pairs, discuss your town/country. Use these ideas to make questions:

mountains *lakes* *industry* *farming*
big towns *museums* *universities* *rain*
sunshine *concert halls* *cold/hot weather*
good films

Example:

Student 1 *How many good museums are there in Paris?*
Student 2 *A lot.*
Student 1 *How much cold weather is there in Japan?*
Student 2 *Not very much.*

START UP

PART B

Look at this cartoon, and discuss with your partner:

1 What is the usual meaning of 'Give me a hand'?
2 Is it formal or informal?

Suggest three different situations in which you could use the phrase.

Function Focus

f

Requests and Offers with *Will* and *Shall*

Will and *shall* are modal auxiliaries.
You know that *will* is often used to express future time.
Example:
What time will you get up tomorrow?
I 'll get up at nine o'clock.
Will also has other very important uses.

Requests and Offers

Requests
Close the door, please.
Will you tidy your room, please?
Will you give me a hand?

Acceptances
Certainly.
(Yes,) of course I will.
Sure.
In a minute.

Refusals
I'm sorry but I'm afraid I can't at the moment.
Sorry!
Sorry, I'm busy now.

Offers
Shall I close the door?
I'll do the dishes.
Shall I give you a hand?

Acceptances
Thank you very much.
(Oh,) thanks.
Thank you so much.

Refusals
It's OK thanks.
It's all right thank you.

PRACTICE

A Look at the sentences in Column A. Match them to the replies in Column B.

The first one has been done for you.

Column A	Column B
1 The dishwasher's broken. **(d)**	**a** Don't worry, I'll help you look.
2 Will you write to Peter or shall I?	**b** It's OK, thanks, I've almost finished.
3 I can't find my purse.	**c** Sorry, I'm using it. I'll give you a lift.
4 Will you mend my shirt, please?	**d** Shall I try and mend it?
5 Will you get me an aspirin, please?	**e** Sure. I'll do it this evening.
6 Lend me a pound, please.	**f** Sorry but I can't. I've only got 50p.
7 Can I borrow your car?	**g** Oh dear. What's the matter?
8 Shall I help you with the cooking?	**h** I will, if you like.

B Cover Column B. Work in pairs, to make dialogues:

Student 1 Read a sentence from Column A, for example, *I can't find my purse.*

Student 2 Make an appropriate response, for example, *Don't worry, I'll help you look for it.*

Student 1 Thank your partner, or, if he refuses your request, say: *Never mind* or *It doesn't matter.*

C In pairs, look at the illustrations. Use the pictures to give you ideas for making requests or offers. Your partner will accept or refuse.

1

2

3

If you refuse, remember to give a reason for refusing, for example, *I'm very sorry, but I haven't got time.*

If your partner accepts, thank him.

If your partner refuses, don't forget to say: *Never mind* or *It doesn't matter.*

PRONUNCIATION

Intonation patterns.

A You will hear some requests. Listen to the intonation and repeat.

B In pairs, use the prompts below to make requests you hear at work. Your partner will accept or refuse.

tidy/desk   *post/letters*   *type/letter*
send/application   *check/train times*

LISTENING

You will hear six short conversations.

A Listen and decide whether the conversations contain a request or an offer.

Tick the appropriate box.

	Request	Offer
1		
2		
3		
4		
5		
6		

B Listen once more, and write down the offers or requests and the responses.

Compare your texts with your partner's.

Example:
Offer: Do you want a hand?
Response: Oh yes. That would be great.

SELF-HELP

A spelling rule: *ie* or *ei*?

The rule is:
i comes before *e* except after *c*.

believe   *field*   *ceiling*

But only when these letters are pronounced like the *ee* as in *meet*.

Look at this list of words. Mark the incorrect ones with a cross.

recieve   *foreign*   *eight*   *reciept*   *hieght*   *thief*
friend   *weight*   *handkercheif*   *belief*   *piece.*

Now look in the dictionary to check your answers.

VOCABULARY BANK

a few   *a little*   *a lot*   *none*   *to paint*
to repair   *to sew*

UNIT 13

PART A

START UP

Look at the illustration.

In pairs, discuss:

1 Which student is working harder than the others?
2 What is she doing?
3 Which student is working carelessly?
4 Why?
5 Which of the students is not doing well?
6 When you don't understand something, what do you do?
7 Using a cassette recorder is one way of improving your English. What are some of the other ways? Which ones do you think work better than others for you?

Grammar Guide

Adverbs

Adverbs describe actions.
Regular adverbs are formed by adding *-ly* to the adjective:

Adjective	Adverb	Example
quick	*quickly*	*He speaks **quickly**.*
beautiful	*beautifully*	*She dresses **beautifully**.*

Adverbs ending in *-y*. Change the *-y* to *-i* before adding *-ly*

easy	*easily*	*They learn **easily***

Here are some irregular adverbs:

Adjective	Adverb	Example
hard	*hard*	*He works **hard**.*
fast	*fast*	*I drive **fast**.*
late	*late*	*You often come **late**.*
good	*well*	*Sleep **well**!*

Comparative Adverbs

There are two ways of using adverbs to make a comparison.

1 *As* + adverb + *as*

Example:
*He learns **as quickly as** his brother.* (Affirmative)
*She doesn't read **as easily as** her sister.* (Negative)

2 Comparative adverb + *than*
Form it like this: *more* + adverb

Adverb	Adverb in comparative form
He learns quickly.	*He learns **more quickly (than** she does).*

Don't forget the irregular adverbs:

Adverb	Comparative form	Example
hard	*harder*	*She studies **harder than** he does.*
fast	*faster*	*Jane learns **faster than** Sally (does).*
late	*later*	*Sam arrived **later than** Harry (did).*
well	*better*	*You speak English **better than** I do.*

PRACTICE

A Maria and her twin brother Carlos are both studying English. Their father is talking to the teacher about their work.

Complete the sentences using the adjectives in brackets to make comparative adverbs:

'They are both good students, and Maria works (1) __________ (hard) __________ Carlos. Carlos is sometimes lazy, and he doesn't read (2) __________ (fast) __________ Maria. Maria writes good essays, but she doesn't write them (3) __________ (good) __________ Carlos. Carlos is lucky; he learns easily. Maria doesn't learn (4) __________ (easy) __________ he does. However she takes a lot of care with her work. She does her exercises (5) __________ (careful) __________ possible.'

B Fill the gaps in the sentences using a comparative adverb:

1 People usually learn a language (good) __________ if they like the course book.
2 Most students study (hard) __________ just before the exams!
3 People sometimes get jobs (easy) __________ if they speak several languages.
4 Students learn a language (fast) __________ if they live in the country where it is spoken.
5 English people think they speak (slow) __________ the French.
6 Some English people think the Italians speak even (fast) __________ the French.
7 Some students learn English (good) __________ from pop songs __________ from a teacher!
8 Some students work (careful) __________ alone __________ in groups.

READING

Are you a good language learner? Do this quiz and you'll find out.

Read each of the questions, and tick *a*, *b* or *c*, whichever is nearest to the truth!

1 When you learn a new word, do you:
a write it in your vocabulary book and revise it the next day?
b repeat it to yourself?
c forget it?
2 You hear a word you don't understand. Do you:
a ask the person to explain it?
b try to guess the meaning?
c smile and say nothing?
3 You see a word you don't know in a newspaper. Do you:
a underline it and look it up in a dictionary?
b guess the meaning?
c look for an easier article?
4 You want to say something difficult. Do you:
a think carefully about what to say before you say it?
b speak immediately, as slowly and as clearly as you can?
c say nothing?
5 When you do your homework, do you:
a re-read what you have written slowly and check for mistakes?
b check your work as you write?
c finish and put your books away quickly?
6 When you're walking along on your own, do you:
a talk to yourself in English?
b think of the English names of things you see?
c think about other things?
7 You come to the bottom of the page of your course book. Do you:
a re-read quickly from the top of the page?
b decide to revise new material later?
c turn the page?
8 Do you write:
a slowly and carefully?
b fast, but you check it afterwards?
c fast and carelessly?
9 When you have an exam do you:
a begin to revise several weeks before?
b revise very hard the night before?
c not revise at all?
10 You find a new grammar point. Do you:
a try to work out what the grammatical rule is?
b say to yourself that you will look it up in your grammar book later?
c leave it, because your teacher hasn't taught it to you yet?

Now count your score. Give yourself: two points for an *a*, one point for a *b*, and no points for a *c*! Total your marks for each question, and look below:

0–6 You work fast and you can learn fast but you could learn faster. You are missing some opportunities to practise English. Work more slowly, and revise as often as you can. You should work more carefully and thoughtfully.

7–13 Good. You learn languages well. You work carefully and study hard. But you can do even better. Learn from your mistakes.

14–20 Excellent! You learn languages easily and well. You speak, listen and write very carefully. You speak clearly and try extremely hard to practise English whenever you can. Well done!

DEVELOPMENT 1

In pairs, discuss the learning techniques described in the questions on page 51, for example, using a vocabulary book, revising, re-reading texts.

1 Do you think they are useful?
2 What do you find helpful when you learn English?

WRITING

A In pairs, discuss and write two more questions for the questionnaire, each with three possible answers. Give your questions to another student to answer.

Look at that student's answers. What sort of language learner is he/she? Tell him/her, and make suggestions about ways to improve his/her language learning.

Heinrich Schliemann, the German archaeologist, discovered Troy. He taught himself to speak and write English, French, Dutch, Spanish, Italian and Portuguese in two years. After that, he taught himself Russian in six weeks. Later, he learnt Swedish, Polish, Latin, Arabic and Greek. He was a polyglot – that means he could speak many different languages.

1 Do you know of any polyglots?
2 How do you think polyglots learn languages?

VOCABULARY

Look at the list of adverbs 1–8. Choose an adverb which has the opposite meaning and fill the gaps.

The first has been done for you.

faster *better* *attentively* *accurately*
easily *fluently* *grammatically*

1 carelessly *carefully*
2 more slowly __________
3 worse __________
4 ungrammatically __________
5 inattentively __________
6 inaccurately __________
7 with difficulty __________
8 hesitantly __________

LISTENING

A There are lots of ways to improve your English.

Listen to the cassette.

Two students are speaking. They are living in the UK and studying English.

Look at the list below,and put a tick in the boxes next to all the ways of learning English that you hear.

□ **1** language schools in your home country
□ **2** language schools in the UK
□ **3** English pen-friends
□ **4** the BBC World Service on radio
□ **5** reading English newspapers
□ **6** English films
□ **7** English boyfriends and girlfriends
□ **8** working as an *au-pair*
□ **9** English magazines and books

B Read the tapescript on page 124 of the Appendices. Listen to the cassette again, and fill in the gaps.

DEVELOPMENT 2

In groups, discuss the following:

1 What do you think is the best way to learn English?
2 How could you make yourselves into better language learners?

PART B

START UP

In pairs, discuss exams.

1 What exams or tests have you taken? (Exams at school or university, for example, or your driving test.)
2 Where did you take them and how long were they?
3 Which were the most difficult, which were the easiest, and why?
4 What exams are you planning to take in the future?

Function Focus

Encouragement

After an exam or an interview, people always want to know what happened.

Look at the following mini-dialogues:

How did you get on? / you do? / it go?

I think I did quite well → *Well done! Keep it up!*

I didn't do very well → *Oh dear, never mind. Keep on trying.*

I messed it up. → *Oh dear. Better luck next time.*

LISTENING

Listen to these five short dialogues in different situations. Fill in the missing information in the chart below.

	1	2	3	4	5
1st Speaker					
2nd Speaker					*Mr Dukes*
Subject				*Contract*	
Formal					
Neutral					
Informal					

PRACTICE

In pairs, make short dialogues like the ones you have just heard. Use the following situations:

1 You have just won a tennis championship. Tell your friend about it. Your friend will respond.
2 You have just taken an important exam. It didn't go well. Tell your friend about it.
3 You have just failed your driving test for the third time. Tell your friend.
4 You went for an interview. You think it went well. Tell another friend about it.
5 The director of the school in which you are studying English has told you to go back to the beginner's class because you are learning very slowly. Tell your friend how you feel.

PRONUNCIATION

English is not pronounced in the same way as it is spelt.

Look at these words:

train *steak* *bathe* *reign*

They are all spelt differently, but the vowel sound is the same.

A **Listen to the cassette and repeat the sound and words you hear.**

B **You will hear a list of words. Each word is numbered. Put the number in the box beside the word you hear.**

The first two have been done for you.

Word	Number
train	
wake	
lake	
bathe	*2*
steak	
stain	
pain	

Word	Number
brain	
make	
take	*1*
reign	
break	
explain	
remain	

C **Now read the words aloud from the list above.**

D **Now listen to the words on the cassette again, and repeat them.**

VOCABULARY BANK

a language learner *to explain* *to guess*
to improve *to look something up* *to repeat*
to re-read *to revise*

UNIT 14

PART A

START UP

Look at the picture.

It shows some common superstitions in England.

1 What are they?
2 Are you superstitious? Tell you partner about your superstitions!

Grammar Guide

If/When* + Present Simple + *Should

(*if* + present simple) + (present modal + verb)
*If you see a shooting star you **should** make a wish.*

*You **should** make a wish **if** you see a shooting star.*
(present modal + verb) + (*if* + present simple)

Other words can be used instead of *if*:
when, after, before, while.

VOCABULARY

Tick the words or phrases which have opposite meanings:

1 backwards:
- a frontwards
- b forwards
- c sideways

2 lucky:
- a unlucky
- b mislucky
- c luckiless

3 tell a lie:
- a tell a truth
- b tell the truth
- c tell truth

4 full moon:
- a empty moon
- b old moon
- c new moon

LISTENING

On the cassette you will hear several friends talking about superstitions.

A Listen and answer the following questions:

1 How many people are talking?
2 How many of them are superstitious?
3 When should you say, 'White rabbits'?
4 Is a black cat lucky?
5 What should you do if you tell a lie?

B Listen to the cassette again and match the sentences below.

1 If you spill salt	a you should say, 'Bless you!'
2 You shouldn't	b you should make a wish.
3 When you see a new moon	c you should walk on the broken pieces seven times.
4 If you break a mirror	d you should turn round three times.
5 On the first day of March	e you should throw some over your shoulder.
6 When someone sneezes	f walk under a ladder.
7 When you see a shooting star	g you should walk downstairs backwards and say, 'White rabbits'.

READING

Do you ever read your horoscope? Do you believe it?

A In pairs, ask your partner what star sign he/she is. Read your partner's horoscope. Tell your partner what he/she should or shouldn't do today. Then ask about members of your partner's family, and tell him/her about their horoscopes.

Capricorn (22 December – 20 January) Today is your lucky day! You will succeed in everything you try. Now is the time to solve any difficult problems and organise your financial affairs.

Aquarius (21 January – 21 February) A good day for friendships – for making new friends and meeting new people. You shouldn't hesitate to speak to people you do not know.

Pisces (20 February – 20 March) A bad day for business - you should not take any important decisions.

Aries (21 March -- 20 April) You should be kind to your family. Do not forget that they need your time and attention as much as your job does.

Taurus (21 April – 21 May) You should think more of yourself and not let others make your decisions for you.

Gemini (22 May – 21 June) Do not spend too much money today. You may want to buy something important, but you should wait till next week.

Cancer (22 June – 23 July) You should organise your life better and spend more time with your family.

Leo (24 July – 23 August) You have forgotten something important. Be careful how you speak today.

Virgo (24 August – 23 September) A good day for making decisions, however big or small.

Libra (24 September – 23 October) Try to control your bad temper. You shouldn't be so quick to criticise other people.

Scorpio (24 October – 22 November) You shouldn't play a sport today. Spend the day quietly at home.

Sagittarius (23 Nov – 21 Dec) Misfortune is very close. Be careful before you accept advice.

B In pairs, ask and answer the following questions:

1 Sue is Capricorn. Should she do business today?
2 Mary is Scorpio. What shouldn't she do today?
3 Sam was born on 25 February. What shouldn't he do today?
4 Who should spend more time with their families?
5 What should Gemini people be careful about today?
6 Sandy's birthday is on 10 October. Should he be less critical of other people?
7 Should Sagittarius people follow advice today?
8 What should Libra people do today?
9 What should and shouldn't you do today?

DEVELOPMENT

There are many different superstitions in different parts of the world. For example, in Japan people think you shouldn't cut your fingernails when the moon is new and in France people think you should cut your hair when the moon is full. In Britain people think it's bad luck to see a new moon through a glass window, but they think a black cat is lucky. In most other countries a black cat means bad luck.

In pairs, discuss:

1 The different superstitions in your country and any others you know of.
2 Why are people superstitious? How did some superstitions begin?

START UP

PART B

Look at this cartoon.

The man is giving his friend a useless piece of advice. Do you know people who often do this? Tell your partner about them. What sort of advice do they give?

Function Focus

The Use of the Modal Verb *Should* for Advice

Strong advice

Look at this dialogue:

George has a problem. He is lonely. He is talking to his friend Jerry about it.

George: *What should I do?*
Jerry: *You should make more friends.*
George: *How can I do that?*
Jerry: *You should go to discos.*

Suggested advice

Now look at the negative form:

Jerry: *Shouldn't you buy some new clothes?*
George: *Yes, I suppose I should. I shouldn't wear these old clothes any more.*

Here are some examples of how to give and accept advice:

Giving advice	Accepting advice
You should work harder.	*Well, maybe you're right.*
I think you should change your job.	*Yes, perhaps I should.*
Shouldn't you go to bed with that cold?	*That's a good idea.*
I don't think you should go to London today.	*Maybe I shouldn't.*
I think you should cut your hair.	*Thanks. I'll think about it.*

PRONUNCIATION

Listen and repeat.

PRACTICE

A **The following five sentences are examples of strong advice about driving. Use the negative question to make each sentence less strong.**

Example:
You should work harder!
Shouldn't you work harder?

1 You should drive more carefully!
2 You should drive much more slowly!
3 You should drive on the left in the UK.
4 You should wear your seat belt .
5 You should stop at the red lights.

B **Work in pairs.**

Use these situations as prompts.

Student 1 Give advice.
Student 2 Reply appropriately.

1 Your friend is trying to play the cassette recorder. He/she has forgotten to plug it in!
2 You have a terrible headache. What does your friend say?
3 Your friend is going to an important interview wearing jeans. What do you say to him?
4 You often borrow your friend's bike. He is fed up with you borrowing his bike. What does he say?
5 Your beautiful friend is looking for a job. You know The Top Class model agency is looking for new faces. What do you say?
6 Your girlfriend/boyfriend has left you and you are very unhappy. What does your best friend say?
7 Your friend's dog is very thin and is always looking for food. What do you say?

DEVELOPMENT

A Here are a few of the problems that many people have at some time in their lives.

In pairs, take it in turns to imagine you have these problems.

Student 1 Give advice.
Student 2 Reply appropriately.

difficulties with mother-in-law *loneliness*
boring, low-paid job with unpleasant boss
horrible children *noisy neighbours*
unreliable car *too much work*

B **In groups of three discuss the best and the worst advice you have ever had. Explain what happened.**

WRITING

Listen to the messages recorded on the answerphone. Make a note of the important points.

1. Meal, Jane + Sam, tomorrow night, 25

2. Sally Barker,

3. Peter,

VOCABULARY BANK

lucky *moon* *star* *wish* *to break*
to make a wish *to sneeze* *to spill*
to tell a lie *to throw*

UNIT 15

PART A

START UP

Look at the map of the treasure island. Fill in the gaps on the map with one of these words:

beach *hole* *jewellery* *coins* *treasure*
cannon *boat* *to dig*

What other kinds of treasure do people sometimes find?

READING

A Look at this photograph. In pairs, discuss the following:

1 What can you see in the photograph?
2 What do you think has just happened?
3 Where do you think he found the object?
4 What do you think the story will be about?

B In groups of three, Students 1, 2 and 3, read these extracts from a magazine article.

It is a true story.

Read your own part of the story only. Do not read the other parts.

Student 1

Simon Burton was thirteen years old and lived in Teignmouth, Devon, with his family. Teignmouth is a pretty town, very popular with tourists. Simon loved swimming and fishing. One evening in July 1975, he went for a swim and began to look for fish. He noticed a large, green, metal object and dived down to see it more clearly. It was about three metres long. He thought it was a cannon and so he swam quickly back to the beach and shouted, 'Hey, Dad! I've found a cannon!'

His father and brother swam back to the cannon with him. They knew the cannon was worth a lot of money, and decided to take it out of the water. They went out the next day in a friend's boat and carefully tied the cannon to the boat. They lifted it gently, and pulled it to the beach. Then they hired a truck to take the cannon home. They put it in the garden because they didn't know what to do next. Simon's father decided to 'phone another friend, who worked in the Customs.

'Simon has just found an old cannon and we've got it in our garden. Should we tell anyone?'

'A cannon? In your garden? Well done! But I'm afraid you must inform this government official. I'll give you his number.'

Student 2

Mr Burton phoned the government official the next morning.

'Hello, my name is Burton, could I speak to Mr Green, please?'

'Jeff Green speaking.'

'Well, Mr Green...' But Mr Green interrupted him.

'Well, Mr Burton, you live in Teignmouth and you found a very old cannon yesterday and you hired a truck to take it to your home and it is now in your garden at 44 Haldon Avenue. Is that what you wanted to say?'

'How did you know?'

'Oh, we know most things. I'll send you a form. Filll it out and send it back to me.'

'What will happen to the cannon?'

'The cannon belongs to the Government. It will go for sale and then you will get some money.'

Student 3

The day of the sale came in November, two years after Simon found the cannon. A lot of people wanted to buy the cannon, including people from Germany and Holland. An Englishman offered the highest price and bought the cannon for £7,000. Simon was very pleased.

'What will you do with the money you get?' a friend asked.

'Well, I'd like to buy a boat.'

'So you want to find more treasure?'

'Well, actually we've already found some. We've found two more cannons. They're in the garden at home.'

Close your books. Tell your part of the story to the other students in your group, starting with Student 1.

C In your groups of three, discuss the following sentences and mark them true (T) or false (F).

Do not re-read the texts until you have tried to answer all the questions.

		T	F
1	Simon was thirteen years old.		
2	The Burtons sold the cannon a few months after they found it.		
3	The government official knew about Simon's find before Mr Burton telephoned him.		
4	Simon found the cannon one afternoon.		
5	If you find some treasure in the sea, you should tell the local Customs office.		
6	An Englishman bought the cannon for £700.00.		
7	The government official wanted Mr Burton to fill in a form.		
8	They left the cannon on the beach.		
9	They found two more cannons after the first.		
10	The Burtons got some money very soon after they found the cannon.		

D Read the first part of the story again. This passage contains five different adverbs. Find them, and underline them.

Are they regular or irregular?

PRACTICE

In your groups, discuss the following questions:

1 What should you do if you find something valuable?
2 If you find a twenty-pound note, do you think you should keep it?
3 Have you ever lost anything valuable? Where and how did you lose it? What did you do to try and find it?
4 Have you ever found anything valuable? What was it, where and how did you find it, and did you tell the Police or a government official about your find?

LISTENING

People use metal detectors to find treasure. The detector makes a noise when it is near metal. Many people have made a lot of money from the treasure they have found: coins, gold, silver, old guns, Roman treasures – these and hundreds of others are under the earth, waiting for someone to find them. Over a quarter of a million people now hunt treasure regularly with metal detectors.

Listen to these true stories told by people who have used a detector and found treasure. As you listen, fill in the chart below.

	What did they find?	How deep was it?	How old was it?	How much was it worth?
Michael Webb	*a wine cup and plate*			
Arthur and Greta			*Roman*	
Edward and David Spiers		*7.5 cm*		

WRITING

Listen to the beginning of the stories again, and fill in the gaps below with the verbs you hear. Think about the tenses of the verbs.

Why are some in the present perfect and others in the past simple?

Story 1

We went to a field. (1) __________ there, but (2) __________ very much, usually just old pieces of iron, sometimes a coin. It (3) __________ late in the evening and (4) __________ to go home. Just then my detector (5) __________ a strong signal.

Story 2

(6) __________ so excited in my life. (7) __________ treasure for many years, and (8) __________ to find something really important. Well, one day (9) __________ in a field in Norfolk. Suddenly I (10) __________ a strong signal.

PART B

Grammar Guide

The Modal Verb *Should*

In Unit 14 we studied the modal verb *should*, used to give advice.

Example:
*You **should** make more friends if you're lonely.*

Should, like *must*, can also be used to express obligation.
Example:
*You **should** close the gate after you. (If you don't, the animals will escape.)*
*You **shouldn't** touch any bombs. (If you do, they may explode.)*

READING

Advice for Treasure Hunters

A Read these don'ts, and match each of the tips to one of the pictures on page 61.

1 Don't leave big holes after you have found your treasure – leave the place as you found it.
2 Don't leave gates open when you cross fields.
3 Don't search other people's gardens.

a

b

c

PRACTICE

Make sentences using *should* and *shouldn't*, using the pictures above.

Example:

You ***should*** *always close gates when you cross fields.*

We also use *should* in the past.

Example:

You ***should have closed*** *the gate after you. (The animals escaped.)*

This is the negative form:

You ***shouldn't have touched*** *any bombs. (You were injured.)*

Make more sentences about the pictures, this time using *should have* and *shouldn't have.*

DEVELOPMENT

Almost every country has treasures – there are the tombs in Egypt, sunken boats around the coasts of Europe, the Caribbean and the West Indies, and the Etruscan tombs in Italy.

In pairs or groups, discuss:

1 What treasure have archaeologists found in your country?
2 Where did they find it, who hid the treasure, and where is it now?
3 Do people steal the treasures in your country?

SELF-HELP

Advice for Writing

Before you write:

1 Think about what you're going to write.
2 Make notes.

When you write:

1 Stop as often as possible and read what you've written.
2 Read from the beginning as often as possible.

After you've written:

1 Go back and re-read.
2 Make changes: put in extra sentences, take out any that repeat what you've already said, change the paragraphing if necessary.
3 Check the punctuation and spelling.

VOCABULARY BANK

beach *coins* *field* *hole* *jewellery*
treasure *to cross* *to dig*

UNIT 16

PART A

START UP

Everybody dreams, but we often forget our dreams when we wake up.
Many people think dreams can tell them about the future.

Look at the illustration.

Maryann is dreaming.

In pairs, discuss these questions:

1 Do you remember your dreams?
2 Do you ever have bad dreams?
3 Tell your partner about a dream you have had.
4 Do you believe dreams can tell you about the future?
5 What is Maryann dreaming about ?
6 Some people think that each of the things Maryann is dreaming about tells something about her future. For example, if she dreams about her stomach, it means that maybe she'll be invited to a meal. What do you think the other things she is dreaming about mean?

Grammar Guide

The First Conditional

The first conditional has two basic forms, as follows:
[*If* + present simple] + *will* and *will* + [*if* + present simple]
Example:
If you dream *about an umbrella* ***you'll*** *become rich.*

You'll *become rich* ***if you dream*** *about an umbrella.*
You can use either the first or the second form – the meaning of the sentence doesn't change.
The first form is used more often for statements.
Example:
If you dream *about an umbrella* ***you'll*** *become rich.*
The second form is used more often for questions.
Example:
What ***will*** *happen* ***if you dream*** *about an umbrella?*

PRACTICE 1

Read this extract from a dream expert's book. Cross out the incorrect grammatical form.

The first two have been done for you.

There are a lot of different ideas about dreams, and many dream experts such as Freud and Jung disagree. Sybil Smith is a dream expert. This is an extract from one of her books:

'A lot of people are afraid of bad dreams. If they (1 eat/~~will eat~~) a large meal before they go to bed, they probably (2 ~~have~~/will have) bad dreams. If they (3 go for a walk/will go for a walk) after their evening meal, they (4 probably have/will probably have) pleasant dreams. Dreams can be frightening, but if you (5 dream /will dream) about death it does not mean someone (6 dies/will die)– it means things (7 change/will change). If you (8 dream/will dream) you are locked in a small, dark place, that means your life (9 changes/will change) for the better. If you (10 are/will be) an open, lively person, you will probably have pleasant dreams. You will dream that you are meeting friends, or helping people. If you (11 are/will be) a quiet person, your dreams (12 are not/will not be) so pleasant. You will dream about things you cannot do or have in real life. Some dreams come true. Most dreams tell us something about the future, if we can understand them.'

LISTENING

Sybil Smith is being interviewed for a radio programme about dreams. She is saying what she thinks different dreams mean.

A Listen to the cassette, and use the information you hear to complete the sentences below.

The first sentence has been completed for you.

1 If you dream about an aeroplane you'll *be lucky*.

2 If you dream about an ambulance you'll __________ .

3 If you dream about an arm you'll __________ .

4 If you dream about biscuits you'll __________ .

5 If you dream about champagne you'll __________ .

6 If you dream about a door you'll __________ .

7 If you dream about jam you'll __________ .

8 If you dream about a stomach you'll __________ .

9 If you dream about traffic you'll __________ .

10 If you dream about an umbrella you'll __________ .

B Compare what Sybil says about the meanings of dreams with your answers from the Start Up exercise.

WRITING

Write a review of the radio programme Sybil Smith is doing. Use this review to help you:

Sunday, 7.30 p.m. Radio 2: *My Life and Work.* Andy Warhol talks about art. The programme is interesting and sometimes surprising. Mr Warhol explains what some of his pictures mean, and why he became an artist. A must for art-lovers!

Begin your review like this:

Saturday, 10.00 p.m. Radio 2: *The Meaning of Dreams.*

PRACTICE 2

A Work in pairs.

Student 1 You are Sybil Smith. Turn to page 124 of the Appendices.

Student 2 You are a radio interviewer. You want to know about the meanings of dreams. Ask Sybil Smith questions such as: *'If you dream about a fish what will happen?'* or *'What will happen if you dream about a fish?'*

B Now ask about the dreams in the picture. Write the meaning of the dreams. After you have asked about the dreams below, ask more questions about dreams.

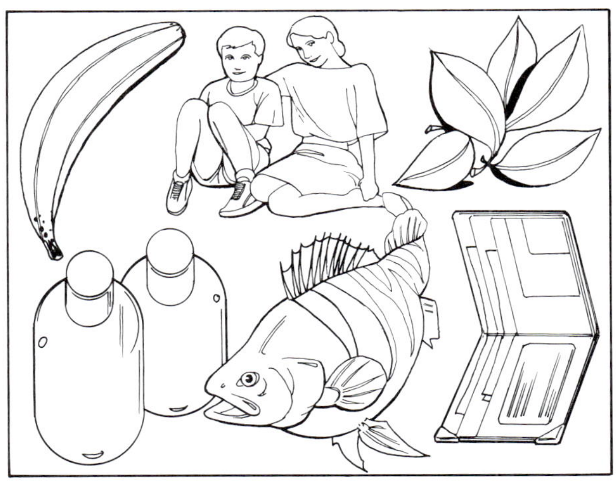

DEVELOPMENT

In groups, discuss:

1 Do you agree with what Sybil Smith says about dreams?

2 Have you ever had a dream come true?

START UP

PART B

Look at the picture.

1 What do you think has happened?
2 What do you think the tramp is saying?
3 What is the bride's reply?

Function Focus

Offers

We have already looked at two ways of making offers in Unit 12:
Example:
1 *Shall I close the door?*
2 *I'll wash the dishes.*

We often use offers in response to exclamations:
Example:
What a heavy bag! ***I'll*** *help you with it* ***if you like.***

Other ways of making offers use the first conditional:
Will + if you want/if you like
Example:
I'll *help you* ***if you want.***
I'll *do the shopping* ***if you like.***

Many exclamations are formed like this:
What a + adjective + noun
Example:
What delicious spaghetti!
What beautiful flowers!

Remember that there is no article before uncountable or plural nouns.

PRACTICE 1

Read these situations. Write an appropriate offer in the spaces.

Example:
Your friend is trying to carry a very heavy case.
I'll *help you with that,* ***if you like.***

1 Your friend doesn't have enough money to go to the cinema with you. You have plenty of money.

____

2 You are at your friend's house. He has lost his glasses.

____

3 There isn't any bread in the house. You are going to the post office, which is near the baker's.

____

4 Your friend can't swim but wants to learn. You can swim.

____

5 Your friend needs to get to the airport, but he doesn't have a car. You have a car.

____

PRONUNCIATION

Listen and repeat.

PRACTICE 2

In pairs, look at the illustrations.

Student 1 Make appropriate exclamations, for example, 'What a beautiful boat!'

Student 2 Make appropriate offers, for example, 'I'll take you for a sail, if you like.'

Student 1 Respond to the offers, for example, 'Oh, thank you very much.'

1

2

3

SELF-HELP

When is it a good time for you to study?

Different people learn best at different times of the day. Some tests show that quiet people learn best in the morning, and lively people learn best in the afternoon. Remember that you don't learn well if you are worried or tired. You learn better if you study a little at a time, not all at once. Think about when and how you personally learn best. Try to study only at your good learning time, and do so for a short time, but often.

Mark the following sentences true (T) or false (F), as appropriate:

		T	F
1	Everybody learns best in the morning.		
2	People learn better if they study for a short time, but often.		
3	You won't learn well if you are worried.		

VOCABULARY BANK

dream *exclamation* *the future* *radio*
to dream *to forget* *to mean* *to remember*
to tell

UNIT 17

PART A

START UP

Look at the illustration.

A foreign student, Suzanne, has just arrived at a student hotel in Los Angeles.

What are some of the things students can and can't do in this hotel?

Make sentences using *can* and *can't*, such as:
They can't smoke.

Grammar Guide

The Modal Verb *Can*

Can is a modal auxiliary. That means it is used to change the meanings of other verbs. (See also Units 3, 12, 14, 15, 23.)

Can has several uses.

1 *Can* (Request):	*'Can you help me?'*	[See Function Focus, page 12, Unit 3.]
2 *Can* (Permission):	*'Can I smoke?'*	[See Function Focus, page 68, this unit.]
3 *Can* (Ability):	*'Can Suzanne speak German?'*	[See Right.]

The present tense of *can* is the same for all persons:

Jane *I **can** speak Russian. **Can** you?*
Maria *No, I **can't** speak Russian, but I **can** speak Polish.*
Jane *Can you really? I **can't**.*

The past tense of *can/can't* is *could/couldn't*:

Paul *Did you post my letter?*
Brian *I'm sorry, I **couldn't** find a post office.*
Paul *But **couldn't** you find a letter box?*
Brian *I didn't have a stamp.*

PRACTICE

A Look at the dialogue between Paul and Brian in the Grammar Guide.

We usually give a reason when we can't do something.

Have short conversations with your partner.

Student 1 Ask if Student 2 did what you wanted.
Student 2 Reply and give a reason.
Student 1 Ask Student 2 another question.
Student 2 Reply and give another reason.

Use these ideas to help you:

1 buy paper / shop closed
2 do homework / no pen
3 get bread / no money
4 light fire / no wood

WRITING

You stayed at this terrible hotel, but you left as soon as you could. Write a postcard about the hotel to a friend. Some lines have been written for you. Write sentences using the prompts below:

Example:
TV – I couldn't watch TV.

1 visitors
2 shower/evening
3 stay in bed/morning
4 stay out/evening

DEVELOPMENT

Talk to your partner about bad hotels you have stayed at and bad holidays you have had.

What couldn't you do?

Here are some ideas to help you:

telephone *breakfast* *money* *sightseeing*
shower *cold drinks* *swim*

LISTENING

Astrid studied English for three months in the UK. She stayed with a British family. She has just returned home. She is telling a friend about her experiences.

Listen and answer:

1 What couldn't she do in her first family? (four things)
2 What couldn't she do with the second family? (one thing)
3 What could she do with the second family? (five things)
4 Have you ever stayed with a British family, or with another family in your own country? What were some of the things you could/couldn't do?

PART B

Function Focus

Asking Permission and Accepting

Could I use your 'phone, please? *Certainly.*
May I use your 'phone, please? *Of course.*

Asking Permission Informally

Is it all right if I use your 'phone? *Sure.*
Is it OK if I use your 'phone? *Go ahead.*

Refusing

Well, actually, I'd rather you didn't + Reason.
Sorry + Reason.
Example:
Could I use your 'phone, please?
Well, actually I'd rather you didn't. I'm waiting for a call from Japan.
Is it OK if I use your phone?
Sorry, I'm waiting for a call from Japan.

PRONUNCIATION

When you ask permission it is important to get the intonation right.

Listen and repeat.

PRACTICE

In pairs:

A

Student 1 You have just started work as a junior secretary in a large office.
Student 2 You are the senior secretary.
Student 1 Ask Student 2 for permission to do various things, using the prompts.
Student 2 Accept or refuse. If you refuse, don't forget to give a reason.

sit here *borrow your pen* *smoke* *switch on the fire* *make a cup of coffee*

B **Now imagine you are in the home of a good friend. Ask permission to do the same things, using informal language.**

READING

A **Look at these pictures.**

1

2

These people are all saying: 'How do you do?' politely. But what exactly are they doing?

Read this text from a magazine article about politeness and write two sentences about each picture. Begin your sentences: ***These people are from... They are...***

Some people think that men were more polite a few years ago than they are now – they opened doors for women, and offered to carry their bags. Women's liberation has changed all that!

Politeness is very important at mealtimes. In the UK, people usually invite guests for dinner at 7.30 p.m. or 8 p.m. They do not expect guests to arrive early, and it's not impolite to be a little late, maybe fifteen or twenty minutes, not more. In Turkey it's very rude to ask guests to come at a certain time. They come whenever they want, early or late. It's also polite to bring a present for your hosts. In the UK, guests usually bring a bottle of wine. In Switzerland, guests often bring flowers, and in Turkey they always bring sweets or chocolates.

It's always polite to ask permission if you want to smoke, or to sit down beside someone you don't know. It's not very polite to refuse permission, unless you have a good reason.

In the UK, it's polite to shake hands when you meet somebody for the first time. In Japan, people don't shake hands, they bow, and in Spain people often kiss each other when they are introduced. In Turkey, men kiss each other when they meet for the first time, and in North Africa and the Middle East people touch their hearts after they shake hands. Eskimos rub noses.

British people often sit with their legs crossed, but in Japan it is very rude to sit in this way.

B Read the passage and mark these statements true (T) or false (F):

The article states that:

	T	F
1 In Japan it is polite to cross your legs.		
2 In Turkey, people invite their friends to dinner at 7.30 – 8 p.m.		
3 People think that men are less polite in the UK than they were.		
4 Eskimos kiss each other when they meet.		
5 It's impolite to arrive early at a dinner party in the UK.		
6 Guests in many countries bring presents for their hosts.		

VOCABULARY

These words are from the reading passage. In the passage, there are also the words which have the opposite meanings. Find those words, and fill the gaps.

1 polite (two possibilities) __________

____

2 guests __________
3 early __________
4 ask permission __________

DEVELOPMENT

1 What is polite or impolite behaviour in your country?
2 Do you think people now are less polite than they were a few years ago?

VOCABULARY BANK

guests hosts impolite polite present to ask permission to invite to kiss to refuse to shake hands

UNIT 18

PART A

START UP

This picture shows a young doctor called Sam Sebastian. He is at work.

In pairs, discuss:

1 What is the matter with the people in the picture?
2 What do these people need? (several things)
3 What help are they getting?
4 The Third World sometimes needs the help of developed countries, because of drought (no rain), or because of war. What other things cause problems in the Third World?
5 Which parts of the world have needed help recently, and why?

Grammar Guide

Linking Words

Function	Linking words	Examples
Contrast	*but* *although*	*There is a little food **but** there isn't enough.* ***Although** there is food in the cities, people in the country are dying of hunger.*
Purpose	*to* *so that*	*Doctors are working hard **to** help the children.* *People are building roads **so that** food can get through*
Result	*so*	*The water is dirty, **so** people are becoming ill.*
Reason	*because* *as*	*People are dying **because** there is no food or water.* ***As** it's winter, the farmers are hoping for rain.*

Remember: *to* is unlike the other linking words – it is part of the infinitive *to help*.

PRACTICE

These sentences are about Sam Sebastian. He works for a charity called Oxfam. Oxfam helps people in the Third World.

Read the sentences and use one of the linking words to fill the gaps.

The first has been done for you.

1 Sam decided to work for Oxfam *because* he wanted to help people.
2 He applied for a job in May __________ he didn't get an interview Until August.
3 The interview was sucessful, __________ he was very nervous.
4 __________ Sam was a qualified doctor, Oxfam sent him to work in a hospital.
5 The hospital was small, and there were many sick people, __________ it was very crowded.
6 He worked hard to help the sick children, __________ many of them died.
7 He needed more helpers and more food __________ make the children well again.
8 He taught mothers about health __________ they could look after their children.

LISTENING

A Listen to the cassette.

1 You will hear two men talking. What are they talking about?
2 What sort of concert are they at?
3 What is the purpose of the concert?
4 Do you have concerts like this in your country? Have you been to one?
5 Charity concerts raise a lot of money for charities. What other activities raise money for charities?

B Read this information about Oxfam.

Sam got it wrong in his talk. What did he say ?

1 Oxfam began over forty years ago.
2 Oxfam supports almost 2,000 self-help projects.
3 These projects are in Africa, Asia, Latin-America and the Middle East.
4 Up to 30,000 people in the Third World die every day because of dirty water.
5 The cost of giving one person clean water is about £2.00.

VOCABULARY

These columns contain words that have opposite meanings.

Join the opposites with a pencil line.

Example:
rich___________poor

1	healthy	a	health
2	to die	b	to live
3	dirty	c	sick
4	war	d	developing countries
5	illness	e	clean
6	developed countries	f	peace

READING

Look at these three photographs.

A In pairs, describe what is happening in each picture.

B Each of the pictures illustrates one of the passages. Read the three passages quickly and decide which one goes with which.

1 In Somalia, the wind is blowing sand onto the fields and so it is difficult for the people to grow enough food. Oxfam is teaching the villagers how to stop the sand. The training courses cost £4.00 per day per person.

2 In Senegal, groups of people are trying to grow food to sell or to feed their families. Oxfam is helping them by giving them equipment. A bucket costs £2.00, a watering can costs £7.80.

3 Oxfam took food to Ethiopia by ship because the situation in that country was so bad. The cost of transport was £114.30 per tonne.

C Mark the following true (T) or false (F):

		T	F
1	A bucket costs £2.00 in Senegal.		
2	Oxfam took food to Ethiopia by ship.		
3	Training courses in Somalia cost £40.00 per week per person.		
4	Transporting food by boat to Ethiopia costs £114.30 per tonne.		
5	Sand is a problem in some parts of Somalia.		
6	In Somalia a watering can costs £7.80.		

START UP

PART B

a

b

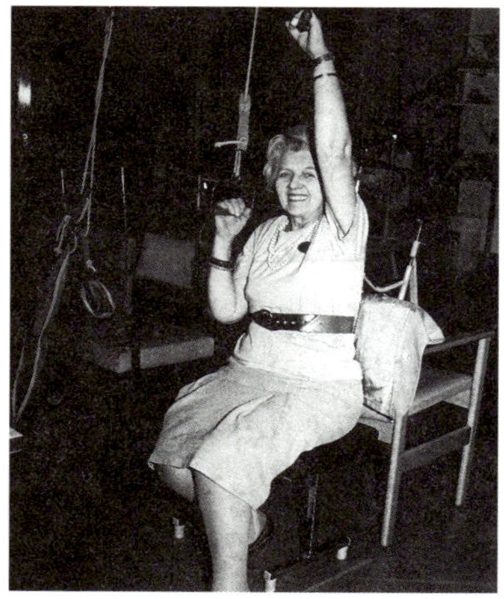

c

A Match the posters to these charities:

1 Oxfam
2 Greenpeace
3 Help the Aged

B In pairs, discuss:

1 What do you think about these charities?
2 Which charities do you support, and why?

Function Focus

f

Asking and Explaining

People will often ask you to explain things. There are many different ways to do this. We often use linking words in explanations.

Look at these questions and answers:

Example:
Why did you do it?
(I did it) because people are dying of hunger.
(I did it) to help people.

Example:
Why should people give money?
(They should give it) because people need it.
(They should give it) to help people.

Here are other ways of asking for and giving explanations.

Asking

Example:
I'm sorry, but I don't understand.
What happened?
Why did you do it?
Can you explain what it's about?
Can you tell me what's going on?

Explaining

Example:
Well, let me explain.
Well, you see, it's like this.
Let me put it this way.
This is how I see it.

PRACTICE

Ask for, and give, explanations. Work in pairs.

Student 1 Begin the conversations in situations 1 – 3. Student 2 respond.

Student 2 Begin the conversations in situations 4 – 6. Student 1 respond.

1 Your friend promised to meet you at the cinema. Nobody came to the cinema, and your friend did not 'phone you. When you see your friend again, ask why.
2 Your friend left a very well-paid job to travel round Europe. You think your friend is crazy. Ask for an explanation.
3 You want to sell your beautiful car to buy a boat. Your girlfriend/boyfriend hates sailing. She/he can't understand you. Explain to her/him.
4 You are a good student. Your teachers want you to go to university. You want to get a job. Explain why.
5 You want to study English in the UK Your family want you to stay in your own country. Explain why you want to go to the UK.
6 Your friend wants to marry someone thirty-five years older than he/she is. You do not understand this at all. Ask your friend about it.

PRONUNCIATION

Listen and repeat.

DEVELOPMENT

Role-Play

The government has decided to give £5,500,000 to three large charities this year. These are the charities:

Greenpeace (The environment of the world.)

Help the Aged (The old people of many countries.)

Oxfam (International help for poor countries.)

In groups of four: Students 1, 2 and 3 are the directors of one of these charities. You each want as much money as possible for your charity. Note down arguments why your charity must have a large share of the money.

Student 4 is chairperson. You must control the meeting, and note down the most important points.

The meeting must continue until everybody agrees on the division of money.

Here are some ideas to help you:

1 Why spend thousands of pounds helping people overseas when there are thousands of people in your own country who badly need help?
2 Why spend money planting trees when there are people dying of hunger?
3 We must protect the environment now or it will soon be too late.

SELF-HELP

Irregular Plural Forms.

Some words do not take *-s* to make the plural form:

1 Words that are the same in the singular and the plural.

Examples:

sheep fish

2 Words that are different in the singular and the plural.

Examples:

foot – feet man– men tooth – teeth mouse – mice

3 Words that have no singular form, but sometimes take a singular verb.

Examples:

news scissors politics trousers mathematics

Cover the examples above.

Look at the following nouns. Are they singular, plural or both. (Write S, S/P or P as appropriate.)

woman sheep politics mice tooth mathematics fish children teeth trousers mouse women news

VOCABULARY BANK

illness peace war to die to fall ill to get better to help to train a course

UNIT 19

PART A

START UP

In pairs, discuss the following questions:

1. Do people often tell jokes and funny stories in your country? When do they usually tell them?
2. The English sometimes tell jokes about the Irish, the Welsh or the Scots. In your country, do you tell jokes about another nationality? Which?
3. What sort of jokes, stories or situations do you think are funny?
4. What do you think of British humour? Is it different from the humour in your country?

Grammar Guide

The Past Continuous Tense

We often use the past continuous tense when we are telling a story. It describes an action or a state that happened in the past over a period of some time.

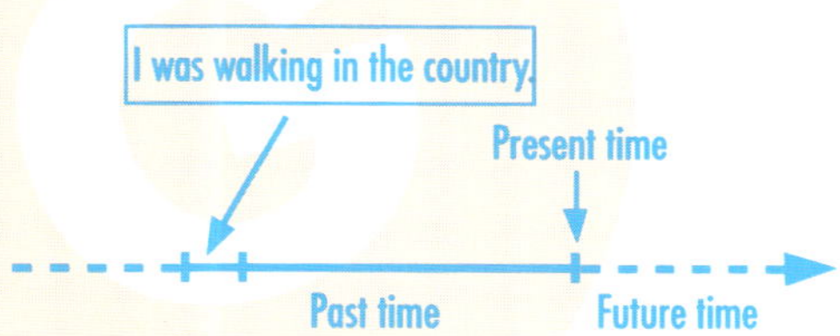

Affirmative form

Pronoun + *was/were* + verb-*ing*

I/he/she/it ***was*** *walking.*

You/we/they ***were*** *speaking.*

Negative form

Pronoun + *was/were* + *not* + verb-*ing*

I/he/she/it ***wasn't*** *walking.*

You/we/they ***weren't*** *speaking.*

Interrogative form

Was/were + pronoun + verb-*ing*?

Was *I/he/she/it walking?*

Were *you/we /they speaking?*

PRONUNCIATION

Listen and repeat.

PRACTICE

We often use the past continuous tense with [*when* + past simple].

Example:

I ***was doing*** *my homework* ***when*** *my friend arrived.* (or ***When*** *my friend arrived I* ***was doing*** *my homework.*)

Join these sentences with *when*. Put the appropriate verb into the continuous tense. Write the sentences.

The first has been done for you.

1 He broke his leg. He played football.
He broke his leg *when* he *was* playing football.
2 He saw the beautiful girl. He sat in the disco.
3 They played tennis. It started to rain.
4 I dropped my wallet. I paid for the book.
5 He knocked at the door. She watched TV.
6 They drove along the motorway. They had an accident.

READING

Read this story. Put the verbs in brackets into the correct tense.

An Englishman was on holiday in Wales. He (1 drive) _________ through the countryside when suddenly his car (2 stop) _________ . He (3 look) _________ round. There weren't any houses near, and there wasn't a telephone. There were only green hills and fields. It (4 rain) _________ and the wind (5 blow) _________. He put on his coat and got out of the car. He (6 look) _________ at the engine when suddenly he (7 hear) _________ a voice.

'Your sparking plugs are dirty.'

The man (8 look) _________ round,surprised. He (9 see) _________ two horses, a white one and a black one.

'Your sparking plugs are dirty,' said the white horse again.

The man looked at his plugs. They *were* dirty. He cleaned them, and started the engine.

He thanked the white horse, and (10 drive) _________ away. When he (11 get) _________ to the next village, he stopped the car. He went into a café and (12 order) _________ coffee.

He spoke to the waiter. He (13 tell) _________ him about the horses.

'Was it the white horse or the black horse that spoke to you?' asked the waiter.

'The white horse,' replied the man.

'That was lucky,' said the waiter, 'the black horse doesn't know anything about cars.'

LISTENING

A Listen to this after-dinner story, told by a writer to a group of friends.

Answer the questions:

1 In the story, the guest that the writer invited was:
a a life insurance salesman
b a film producer
c his wife
2 The film producer ate:
a steak
b pudding
c fish and chips

B Listen again, and mark these statements true (T) or false (F) with a tick:

	T	F
1 The writer was writing his second novel.		
2 The producer was thinking about buying the film rights of his first novel.		
3 The producer was driving down from Oxford.		
4 The producer was hoping to impress the writer.		
5 The writer and his wife were laying the table when the producer arrived.		
6 The writer was eating pudding when the doorbell rang a second time		

START UP

PART B

a b c

Look at the cartoon.

What is the correct order of the pictures?
Number them 1, 2 or 3.

Function Focus

f

Story Telling

All stories and a lot of sentences have a beginning, a middle and an end. When we tell a story, we sometimes need to show which action happened first, and which actions happened afterwards. These are some of the words we can use. They are called adverbials:

The Beginning	The Middle	The End
first	*then*	*finally*
first of all	*and then*	*in the end*
at first	*after that*	*at last*

WRITING

Now use these phrases to help you write out the cartoon story. Work in pairs.

a man and a woman *very tall and fat*
small umbrella *under the umbrella*
getting very wet and annoyed *other side of the man* *still getting very wet* *bucket of water*
very surprised

PRACTICE

A The following sentences tell a story, but they have been mixed up. Put them in the right order, by filling in the boxes below.

a b c d e f

Sentence 1 is the beginning:

1 A man was on his way home from work. He was very tired and hungry. [*a*]

2 He sat down and started eating. First he ate everything on his plate and then he finished the food in the dish. Finally, he stopped. [ ]

3 'Well, actually Mr Baggins, we have. You're in the wrong house. You live next door.' ☐
4 'Mmm! potato omelette' he said. 'That was delicious! Why haven't we had it before?' ☐
5 When he got home he put down his case and took off his coat. After that, he went into the dining room. ☐
6 The woman who was sitting on the other side of the table finally looked up. ☐

B **Look at this part of the story again:**

He sat down and started eating. First he ate everything on his plate and then he finished the food in the dish. Finally, he stopped.

Use the adverbials from the Function Focus to complete the following sentences:

1 He put down his case. He took off his coat. He went into the dining room.
2 He drove to the station. He got on the train. He fell asleep.

Now try these:

3 Mix the eggs with the flour. Add a little sugar. Put it in a hot oven.
4 I'll work on a ship. I'll have a long holiday. I'll come home.
5 We have a pizza. We usually go to the cinema. We go to a disco or a night-club.

VOCABULARY

Tick the correct word or phrase.

1 a to say a joke
b to tell a joke
c to speak a joke
2 a a funny story
b a fun story
c a joke story
3 a a sense of funny
b a sense of joking
c a sense of humour
4 a dead funny
b alive funny
c disfunny

DEVELOPMENT

Funny programmes on television are called comedy programmes or comedies.

1 What sort of comedy programmes are there on the television in your country?
2 Do you enjoy watching comedies?
3 What are comedies often about?
4 Have you seen any comedy programmes in the UK? How are they different from comedies in your own country?

VOCABULARY BANK

comedy *finally* *first* *funny* *humour* *a joke* *to laugh* *to tell a joke* *a funny story* *then*

UNIT 20

PART A

START UP

A In pairs, talk about your first English lesson:

1 What did you learn?
2 Could you understand everything?
3 Which parts of the lesson were easiest?
4 What did you find difficult?

B Discuss your language learning now:

1 What do you find easiest to learn? Why?
2 What do you find most difficult? Why?
3 What helps you understand and remember what you learn? For example, making pictures of things in your head to help you remember their names.
4 In which areas of language learning do you need to work hardest? For example, grammar, pronunciation, writing, speaking, spelling, vocabulary.

VOCABULARY

These words are about learning languages. Use them to fill the gaps in the sentences.

practise revise accent guess improve correct

1 He spoke with a very strong French __________ so I couldn't understand him.
2 If you aren't sure about the meaning of a word, you should try to __________ it.
3 If you __________ your English, you'll __________ it.
4 If you make a mistake, try to __________ yourself.
5 You should __________ everything you have learnt before you take a test.

READING

How to be a Good Language Learner

A The six sentences describe what a good language learner does. Each of the sentences summarises one of the paragraphs a–f. Match the sentences to the paragraphs

The first sentence has been done for you.

Good language learners:

1 develop self-help techniques. (c)
2 try to think in the language.
3 do various activities to help them learn English.
4 feel confident about learning the language.
5 know that language is for communicating.
6 guess.

a Good language learners know that learning a language needs time. They try to be confident. They do not give up. They keep trying.

b Good language learners know that if they think in the language, they will learn faster and better.

c Good language learners think carefully about the language. They develop techniques to improve their pronunciation, grammar and vocabulary. For example, when they learn new words, some learners make a picture of the object in their heads.

d Good language learners develop techniques for listening carefully, speaking fluently, reading quickly and writing grammatically. At first they do not worry much about making mistakes. They try to communicate as much as possible, and they try to speak fluently. They speak with native speakers as often as they can.

e Good language learners make guesses and ask people to correct their mistakes. They compare what they say with what other people say. They note down what they have learned and think about it.

f Good language learners go to language classes. They also do other activities to help them learn, such as watching English films, or buying English books and magazines. They choose the activities carefully, either to help them with special problems, or to revise what they already know. They practise as often as they can.

B The sentences in the next column are about the text. Some are true, some are false. Read them, check the text, and mark them T or F:

Good language learners:

		T	F
1	never guess.		
2	sometimes make pictures in their heads to help them remember.		
3	always worry about making mistakes.		
4	do not ask other people to correct them.		
5	compare what they say to what other people say.		
6	do language activities outside the classroom.		
7	give up quickly and stop trying.		
8	try to think in the language.		
9	try to talk as much as they can.		
10	never need to make notes.		

DEVELOPMENT

Read the paragraphs a–f again. In pairs, discuss:

1 Do you agree with these ideas about language learning?
2 Do you do some of the things that are in the article?
3 What don't you do? Why not?
4 What should you (personally) do to become a better language learner?

LISTENING

A A group of foreign students are in the coffee bar at their school. They are talking about their experience of language learning, the problems they have and their reasons for learning English. You will hear several short dialogues.

Listen and answer these questions:

Dialogue A

1 Where was Heinz studying before?
2 Does he like the school he is in now better than the one he was in before?

Dialogue B

1 Could Abdullah speak any English when he got here?
2 Could Ahmed speak any English?

Dialogue C

1 Why is Fumie learning English?
2 Where was she studying English before she came to the UK?

Dialogue D

1 Is Akiko enjoying her course?
2 Why doesn't she want any homework?

B Listen again. As you listen, fill the gaps:

1 I (a) __________ in London but I (b) __________ only have four lessons a day and I (c) __________ use the learning centre after my lessons. I wanted six lessons a day, (d) __________ I changed schools and came here.

2 I (a) __________ a word. I (b) __________ even (c) __________ 'Good morning.'

3 Sure – I (a) __________ there, but my teachers were Japanese (b) __________ I (c) __________ improve my accent.

4 Yes, very much, (a) __________ I do miss my friends and my family – and good food!

START UP

1

2

Look at the pictures.

They show two of the ways students use the English they learn.

1 What are the two ways?
2 Are you learning English to use it in one of these ways? Which one?

PRACTICE

In Picture 1, the two businessmen have just met. They are using English for business. They are speaking formally. In Picture 2, a married couple are using English to help them travel. They are speaking informally.

A In the sentences below, people are asking, refusing and giving permission. Read the sentences. Who are speaking, the businessmen or the couple? Mark the sentences *B* if you think it's the businessmen or *C* if you think it's the travelling couple.

1 Could I possibly use your 'phone, please?
Yes, certainly.
2 OK if I borrow your umbrella?
Sure.
3 May I look at your newspaper, please?
Of course.
4 Is it all right if I put this here?
Go ahead.
5 May I smoke, please?

Well, actually, I'd rather you didn't, this is a no-smoking office.

B Cover the exercise above.

Work in pairs.

Student 1 Ask your partner for permission to:
sit here *make a coffee* *use the telephone*
smoke

Student 2 Refuse or give permission. Don't forget to give a reason if you refuse permission.

C Look at these offers, acceptances and refusals. Are they formal or informal? Mark each pair of sentences F (formal) or I (informal), as appropriate.

1 Shall I send you a copy?
Oh, thank you so much.
2 I'll do it, if you like.
It's OK, it won't take a minute.
3 I'll ask the boss.
Thank you very much.
4 I'll get it for you, if you want.
Thanks.
5 Shall I arrange a meeting?
Thank you, but it's all right, I can do it.
6 I'll do the shopping, if you like.
It's OK, thanks, I'll do it.

D Cover section C.

Work in pairs.

Student 1 Make offers using the following prompts:
show you our new office *do the dishes*
introduce you to our boss *get some stamps*
dig the garden *arrange an interview*

Student 2 Accept or refuse.

VOCABULARY BANK

accent *correct* *guess* *improve* *practise*
revise

UNIT 21

PART A

START UP

A **Look at the picture.**

The year is 1890.

In pairs, discuss the following questions:

1 Who are all the people in the picture?
2 How was life different then from life now? (At least three things.)

B Which of the following things do you think existed at that time?

Write *yes* or *no* beside each thing.

1 Newspapers
2 Telephones
3 Bicycles
4 Cars
5 Cameras
6 Television
7 Trains
8 Dishwashers
9 Electricity
10 Gas ovens

Grammar Guide

Used To

Use to/Used to describes habitual actions in the past.
It describes actions or events which no longer happen.

Affirmative	Negative	Interrogative
I used to...	*I didn't use to...*	*Did you use to...?*
	I never used to...	*Did you ever use to...?*
There used to be...	*There didn't use to be...*	*Did there use to be...?*
	There never used to be...	*Did there ever use to be...?*

Example:

There used to be more illness.
This means: *There is less illness now.*
Women used to wear long skirts.
This means: *They don't wear long skirts now.*

Now look at the negative:

*Women **didn't use to** wear trousers.*
This means: *They do wear trousers now.*
*Women **never used to** smoke.*
This means: *They do smoke now.*

PRONUNCIATION

Listen and repeat the words and phrases.

VOCABULARY

In pairs, look at these words:

dishwasher gas politician central heating
scientist fridge washing machine writer
nuclear oven artist vacuum cleaner
electricity poet open fire

Discuss their meanings and divide them into groups under the following headings:

Professions *Equipment for the house*
Keeping warm *Means of power*

PRACTICE 1

A **Now answer these questions, like this:**

Example:
When you were a child, what did you use to do?
I used to play with my toys.
Now you do it:

1 When you were a child, what kinds of things did you use to play with?
2 When you were about ten, what food did you use to like?
3 When you were about fourteen, what did you use to wear?
4 When you were a bit younger, where did you use to go on holiday?
5 When you were about twelve, what time did you use to go to bed?

B Think about how rich families and their servants lived in Victorian England.

Make questions and answers like this:

Question *What/do/evening?*
Answer *Books*
Question *What did they use to do in the evening?*
Answer *They used to read books.*

1 Question: How/contact friends? Answer: letters
2 Question: How/wash clothes? Answer: by hand
3 Question: How/keep warm? Answer: open fires
4 Question: What/wear? Answer: Tight, heavy clothes
5 Question: How/clean the house? Answer: brushes

Now ask these questions using a different form:

1 Question: Did/travel by train?
2 Question: Did/have fridges?
3 Question: Did/ride bicycles?

Now think of five more questions to ask about how the Victorians used to live.

LISTENING

You will hear a discussion between two friends about whether life is better now than it was in Victorian England.

Listen and make a list of the advantages and disadvantages of life as it used to be:

Advantages	Disadvantages

PRACTICE 2

The negative form of *used to* is *didn't use to/never use to.*

Example:
Victorian women ***didn't use to*** *wear bikinis.*
In pairs, look at the five pictures below and make a negative sentence about each one. Now think of five more things they didn't use to do in Victorian England. Write them down and then compare them with your partner's.

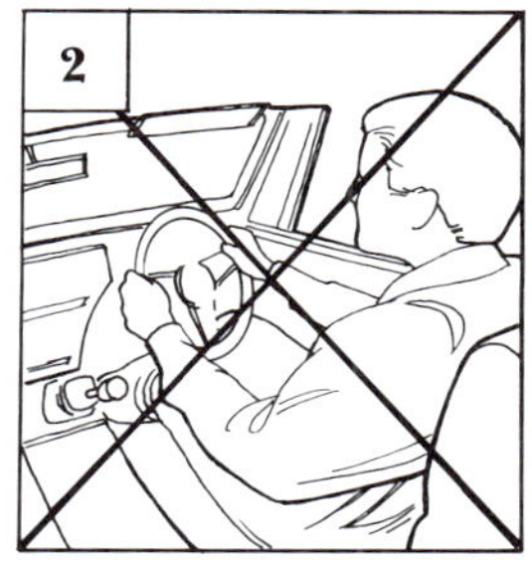

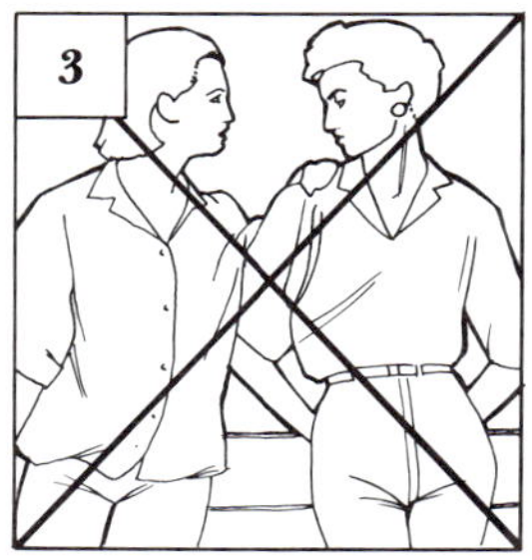

WRITING

Do you think life is better now than it used to be? Think about life in your own country, and in your own family.

Ask your partner how his/her life is different from the life of his/her great-grandparents or grandparents. Write your partner's comments in two columns, under advantages and disadvantages.

Do you agree with him/her?

START UP

a

b

Look at this information about the lives of some important Victorians.

Who are the people in the photographs?

1 Charles Dickens (1812–1870) Began life poor, but became the most popular writer of the nineteenth century. He wrote *Oliver Twist*.

2 Prince Albert (1819–1861) The Consort of Queen Victoria. They got married in 1840. He died in 1861. The Queen wore black for the rest of her long life.

3 Sir Arthur Conan Doyle (1859–1930) The doctor who created the world-famous characters of Sherlock Holmes and Dr Watson. His most famous book is *The Hound of the Baskervilles*.

4 Benjamin Disraeli (1804–1881) Prime Minister twice, and friend of Queen Victoria.

5 Oscar Wilde (1854–1900) Irish writer, poet and playwright. He set the fashions in society with his long hair and colourful ties.

6 Queen Victoria (1819–1901) She came to the throne in 1837, when she was just a girl, and ruled Britain for over sixty years. She asked the man she loved, Prince Albert, to marry her. He agreed and they were married in 1840.

7 Charlie Chaplin (1889–1977) The first international film star. Born at the end of the Victorian age, his parents were poor theatre artists. He went into the theatre for the first time when he was five years old.

8 Emmeline Pankhurst (1858–1928) A brave woman who fought for the liberation of women, and for their right to vote.

9 William Gladstone (1809–1898) Entered Parliament in 1832, and was Prime Minister for over fifteen years.

10 Florence Nightingale (1820–1910) A British nurse. She went to nurse British soldiers wounded in the wars overseas.

11 Charles Darwin (1809–1882) The scientist who wrote *The Origin of Species*. This was the first time the theory of the evolution of species was put forward. Many scientists of the day agreed with him, but he was very unpopular with the Church.

READING

Read the passages again, and fill the gaps:

Queen (1) __________ and her husband (2) __________ enjoyed many years of peace. The Victorian Age was famous for its writing. Two of the best-known writers were (3) __________ and (4) __________ . The Victorians often went to the theatre, and particularly enjoyed the plays of (5) __________ . Parliament was dominated by the two great politicians of the time, (6) __________ and (7) __________ . There were no women in Parliament, in fact, women didn't even have the right to vote, until (8) __________ won them the right. Another famous woman of the time was (9) __________ whose work as a nurse earned her the title: 'The Lady of the Lamp.'

Function Focus

When we listen to people, we usually show our interest in what they are saying.
We show interest verbally (with words) and non-verbally (with sounds).

Non-Verbal Interest

We use sounds very often to show our interest.

Example:
Mmmhmm?
Aha?
Oh!

Verbal Interest

We often show interest by using short answers (an auxiliary verb and a pronoun).

Example:
He used to live in Shanghai.
Oh, did he?
I want to visit New York.
Do you?
I'm studying Japanese.
Are you?
I've met the Queen.
Oh, have you?

PRACTICE

Show your interest!

Example:
Speaker 1 *I've just seen a film.*
Speaker 2 *Oh, have you?*
Now continue with your partner.

1 **Student 1** I've just seen a film.
Student 2 ______________________________
2 **Student 1** Yes, it was on in the ABC cinema.
Student 2 ______________________________
3 **Student 1** It was very long.
Student 2 ______________________________
4 **Student 1** It lasted three hours.
Student 2 ______________________________
5 **Student 1** It isn't very good.
Student 2 ______________________________
6 **Student 1** It's about life in the last century.
Student 2 ______________________________
7 **Student 1** Conditions were very hard.
Student 2 ______________________________
8 **Student 1** People didn't have electricity.
Student 2 ______________________________
9 **Student1** And they couldn't travel fast.
Student 2 ______________________________
10 **Student 1** They used to die quite young.
Student 2 ______________________________

DEVELOPMENT

In groups, talk about the famous people who lived in the nineteenth century in your country.

1 Were they politicians, writers, army leaders, scientists, poets?
2 What did they do?

Don't forget to show interest in what your partner says.

VOCABULARY BANK

century electricity fridge gas oven politician scientist writer to clean to contact to keep (warm)

UNIT 22

PART A

START UP

A Look at this picture. In pairs, discuss the questions:

1 What are the different items in the picture? What are they for?
2 Which bank or banks do you use? What do you use them for? How often do you go to a bank? Do you get letters from your bank ? What about?

B Use the words below to fill the gaps in the picture:

a traveller's cheque *the cashier* *a form* *cash*
a cheque *foreign currency* *a Eurocheque*

Grammar Guide 1

Multi-Word Verbs

We often use multi-word verbs in English.
A multi-word verb can be a:

Verb +	**Place Adverb**
to turn	*on*
to sit	*down*
to get	*up*
to take	*off*
to find	*out*

Multi-word verbs often take an object.
The object can be:

1 A noun object.
Example:
*He **turned on** the light.*
or
*He **turned** the light **on**.*

2 A pronoun object.
Example:
*He **turned it on**.*
Remember: multi-word verbs do not always take an object:
*He **took off** his hat.* [+ object]
*The plane **took off**.* [no object]

PRACTICE 1

A Underline the multi-word verbs in the following sentences.

The first has been done for you.

1 *The manager <u>turned</u> the computer <u>on</u>.*
2 The millionaire smiled unpleasantly as he wrote out the cheque.
3 He paid the cheques in.
4 Take off your coat and sit down. The manager will see you in a minute.
5 First of all, just fill in this form, please.
6 Give out the application forms today.
7 Find out the facts, Inspector. I want those robbers caught!
8 I don't know what to do. I have to pay back the money tomorrow but I can't!
9 Throw this cheque away and start again. You made a mistake.
10 Write the cheque number down for me, please.

B Rewrite the same sentences, using a pronoun object instead of a noun object.

The first has been done for you:

1 The manager turned it on.

Grammar Guide 2

Multi-Word Verbs

Some multi-word verbs take an adverb and a preposition:

A Verb +	A Place Adverb +	A Preposition
to look	*forward*	*to*
to catch	*up*	*with*
to put	*up*	*with*
to get	*away*	*with*
to stay	*away*	*from*
to check	*up*	*on*
to cut	*down*	*on*

With these verbs, always put the object after the preposition:

Verb	Place Adverb	Preposition	Object
I am looking	*forward*	*to*	*the weekend.*
The robber got	*away*	*with*	*£5,000.*
Police caught	*up*	*with*	*him.*

PRACTICE 2

These sentences have been mixed up. Unscramble them!

1 expenses/wants to cut /The company/down on
2 He's dangerous. /from/away/him/Stay
3 He's a useless politician. /him/why we put/I don't know/up with /
4 checked/ the/ The detective/bank employee/ up on/
5 I'm so tired./ looking forward/I'm really /a good holiday /to /

READING

A Read these true stories about banks, and match them to the headlines:

a *The Hamburger Robber*
b *The Two Mr Zs*
c *The Robber who Slipped Up*
d *The Robber who was Sorry*

Story A

An Italian bank robber fell over the doormat as he ran into a bank in Milan. As he fell, his **mask** fell off. He tried to cover his face, but he dropped his gun. The gun went off but did not **injure** anyone. He got up, and ran towards the **counter.** Then he slipped on the floor and fell once more. He dropped his gun again. By this time everyone in the bank was laughing. The robber turned and ran out, red with **embarrassment.** He ran straight into the arms of a policeman who was writing him a ticket. The robber's car was parked **illegally.**

Story B

A robber went into a bank in Davenport, Tasmania, pulled out a gun, put a bag on the counter and ordered the cashier to fill the bag with money. She was putting in everything she had when the robber said,

'That's enough.'

He left with about £5,000.

A few minutes later, he came back. He put the bag back on the counter.

'I'm sorry, I didn't really mean to rob you,' he said. He then waited for the police to arrive.

Story C

A nine-year old boy walked into a bank in New York, pulled out a toy gun, and walked out with $100. He was so small the security cameras didn't see him. He spent $80 on hamburgers, chips and a watch, and he went to see three films at the cinema. Then he went to a police station and gave himself up. His lawyer said the boy often used to watch crime shows.

Story D

An American bank employee programmed the bank's computer to 'lose' 10 cents each month from every client's account and add it to the last account. The bank employee then opened an account with a name beginning with 'Z'. All went well and the employee received a lot of money month after month. Then a man with a real name beginning with 'Z' opened an account. His name was even further down the alphabet, and so he began to receive all the extra money. He 'phoned the bank to ask why...

B **Work in groups of three. Student 1 read Story B, Student 2 read Story C, Student 3 read Story D. Read the stories carefully. Then close your books and take it in turns to tell the stories to your group.**

C **As you listen to the stories, complete this form:**

Questions	Story B	Story C	Story D
1 Was the robber a child or an adult?			
2 Did the robber use a gun or a computer?			
3 Did he steal a lot of money or only a little?			
4 Was the robber caught?			

SELF-HELP

Read Story A slowly. What do the words in bold type mean? Do not use your dictionary! Guess the meanings from the rest of the story, and circle the correct definition of the words:

1 mask:
a a kind of hat
b something to hide the face
c trousers
2 injure:
a touch
b hurt
c frighten
3 counter:
a a piece of furniture
b a kind of counting machine
c an exit
4 embarrassment:
a anger
b fear
c shame
5 illegally:
a without a ticket
b against the law
c badly

PRONUNCIATION

Listen and repeat.

PART B

START UP

1 What sort of forms do you sometimes fill in?
2 What sort of information must you give?
3 Do you like filling in forms? Why? Why not?

WRITING

You are going to go abroad for a month on a trip to three countries. You are travelling by train and staying in hotels. Decide which three countries you want to go to and fill in Form A.

FunctionFocus

Filling in Forms

You will often find the words and phrases in Column A on forms. Match them to the items in Column B.

Column A	Column B
1 Postcode	a Smith
2 Please tick	b M. A.
3 Surname/family name	c Please debit my / ~~our~~ account
4 Initials	d ABCDEFG...
5 Delete as appropriate	e Mary Anne
6 First names/forenames	f PS45 6NW
7 Capital letters	g ✔

a

Western Bank Plc Service application form

Mr, Mrs, Ms

Initials

Surname

Address

Tel no Postcode

Foreign currency notes

Country	Amount of foreign currency	or	Sterling equivalent

Sterling travellers cheques

Available for use in all countries throughout the world, but travellers in North and Latin America and the Philippines are advised to take travellers cheques expressed in US Dollars

Name of person signing cheques

Number required		Value
	of £10 each	
	of £20 each	
	of £50 each	
	of £100 each	

Declaration

Please delete as appropriate

-Please debit my account number

Account holding branch

-I undertake to provide payment by: Access/Visa/Mastercard/American express/Diners card

Account name

Card number

Customer signature

Date

LISTENING

Your friend Jane is going abroad on holiday. You are with her now in a bank. She wants to order some money to take with her.

Listen to her conversation with the bank cashier and fill in Form B on page 125 of the Appendices for her.

DEVELOPMENT

1 What stories do you know about banks and bank robbers?
2 Have you or your friends ever had any problems with your accounts at the bank?
3 Do you think banks do a good job, or could they do better?

VOCABULARY BANK

cash cashier cheque foreign currency
form initial surname traveller's cheque
to fill in to find out to pay back to rob
to throw away to write down/out

UNIT 23

PART A

START UP

Look at the picture. In pairs, discuss:

1 What sort of shop is this, and what does it sell?
2 Do you sometimes go to shops like these? What interests you?
3 The man in the picture is a collector. He collects paintings. Do you collect anything? What do you collect?
4 Why is the man looking at the picture so carefully?

VOCABULARY

Put these words into the columns, as appropriate:

antique shop *drawing* *collector* *art gallery*
antique *artist* *picture* *museum* *painter*

People	Places to see art	Works of art

Grammar Guide

May/Might

May and *might* are both modal auxiliaries. That means they are used to change the meanings of other verbs. (See also units 3, 12, 14, 15, 17.)
They are almost the same in meaning, and they have several uses. In Unit 17 we saw that *may* is used for asking permission. In this unit we will learn to use it for expressing uncertainty.

Structure	May	Might
Affirmative:	*I/you/he **may** buy the painting.*	*I/you/he **might** buy it.*
Negative:	*I/you/he **may not** buy the painting.*	*I/you/he **mightn't** buy it*
Affirmative:	*It **may** be a Picasso.*	*It **might** be a Picasso.*
Negative:	*It **may not** be a Picasso.*	*It **mightn't** be a Picasso*
Affirmative:	*There **may** be a signature on it.*	*There **might** be a signature on it.*
Negative:	*There **may not** be a signature on it.*	*There **mightn't** be a signature on it.*

Meaning:
He may/might = It's possible but I really don't know.
May and *might* have both a present and a future meaning.
He may/might be at home = It's possible that he's at home now.
He may/might go to Japan = It's possible he will go to Japan in the future.

PRACTICE

A You are with a friend in a junk shop. Use the prompts to make dialogues like the following:

Picasso/copy

Student 1 *I think it's a Picasso.*

Student 2 *It may not be. It may be a copy.*

1 valuable/valueless
2 old/recent
3 Chinese/Japanese
4 nineteenth century/twentieth century
5 Van Gogh/copy
6 exciting find/bit of rubbish

B In pairs, look at these pictures.

b

a

They are the work of two of the artists listed. Which ones?

Botticelli Vermeer Goya Van Gogh Gaugin Velazquez Rembrandt Leonardo da Vinci Michelangelo Rubens Picasso Dali Cézanne Chagall El Greco Turner

Discuss the pictures, and use language such as: ***Well, it might be a Botticelli... No, I don't think so. I think the artist may be Leonardo da Vinci.***

Write the artists' names below the pictures.

READING 1

Turn to page 125 in the Appendices. Read the extracts from an art catalogue and match the descriptions to the pictures.

WRITING

Continue the short description of the paintings. Write three more sentences for each painting.

READING 2

A These paragraphs are out of order. They tell the story of the man in the picture at the beginning of the unit. Discuss with your partner what you think the story might be about.

B Now read the paragraphs and put them in the right order.

The first one has been done for you:

1 e **2** **3** **4** **5**

a I couldn't believe my eyes. I kept looking and looking at it. I had to buy that picture. I tried to look calm. I asked the price. She said £100. Now that's a lot of money. But I didn't argue, I wrote a cheque, picked up the painting and almost ran for the door.

b I nearly found a valuable painting the other day. I was driving around Birmingham, in a part of the city where I thought there might be junk shops. It started to rain, so I decided to go home. Just then, I saw a junk shop, so I parked the car. It was a lovely old junk shop, full of interesting things. I went in, and started looking through their paintings.

c Outside, in the street, I remembered my umbrella. It was still in the shop. I went back. The shop assistant didn't hear me go in. She was shouting to somebody through a door in the back of the shop:

'Albert? Are any of those Picassos dry yet? We need another in the front.'

d It was all the usual old rubbish. Then, at the back of the pile, there was a painting that caught my eye. It was in the style of Picasso. It's unusual to find modern pictures in junk shops, but there it was. I looked at it more closely. It looked very like a Picasso. The colours he used, the lines, the shapes – everything was in the style of Picasso.

e I've been collecting paintings for a long time now. I love art and I find going round the junk shops very exciting. You never know what you might find. You may be lucky and come across something quite valuable, which you can buy for a few pounds and then sell for thousands. I hope one day that might happen to me, so I'm always looking for paintings that may be valuable.

DEVELOPMENT

There are many different art forms: painting, architecture, music and dance are some examples.

1 Which of the different art forms do you like best, and why?
2 Which ones don't interest you?
3 How often do you go to museums, galleries or other places where you can enjoy art?
4 Do you think some famous pictures are overpriced?

START UP

PART B

In pairs, look at the picture.

Is the girl's face:

- **a** hopeful
- **b** doubtful
- **c** thoughtful
- **d** beautiful
- **e** thankful

Function Focus

Expressing Doubt and Uncertainty

The following structures show that we are uncertain about things:

might /might not:	*It **mightn't** be sunny tomorrow, it **might** rain.*
may /may not:	*I **may** go to the party, but I **may not** stay very long.*

The following phrases also show that we are uncertain. We often use them with the structures above:

Well, I'm not really sure:	*I **might** see him tonight, but **I'm not really sure...***
I don't know for certain:	*He **may** be coming, but **I don't know for certain.***
I'm not sure/certain:	*That **might** be the right answer, but **I'm not sure...***
I doubt it:	*He **might** pass the exam, but **I doubt it.***
I don't think so:	*That horse **might** win the race, but **I don't think so.***

PRONUNCIATION

We usually stress *may* and *might* rather than the main verb.

Listen and then listen and repeat.

Note the intonation.

PRACTICE

In pairs, look at the following prompts.

Student 1 Make questions. Remember to use the present continuous with future meaning.
Student 2 Answer, using expressions of doubt.

The first has been done for you:

1 go out/Friday night?

Student 1 *Are you going out on Friday night?*
Student 2 *I might, but I don't know for certain.*

2 go/cinema/weekend?
3 meet your friends/Saturday afternoon?
4 have a party/on your birthday?
5 buy/new clothes next week?
6 pasta/supper?
7 go for a walk/weekend?
8 play football/on Sunday?

LISTENING

A **You will hear eight short dialogues. Three of these match the situations in the pictures below. Put the number of the dialogue beside the letter of the corresponding pictures.**

B **In the Function Focus, tick the expressions of doubt or uncertainty that you hear on the cassette.**

a

b

c

DEVELOPMENT

In Unit 21, you talked about how your life is different from that of your grandparents and great-grandparents. How different do you think life might be for your grandchildren and great-grandchildren? You could talk about:

food *houses* *transport* *technology*
education *jobs* *holidays* *medicine*
politics *religion*

VOCABULARY BANK

art *artist* *collection* *copy* *museum*
painting *picture* *to collect* *to copy*
to paint

UNIT 24

PART A

START UP

Grammar Guide

To make = to force.

Example:
In the Marines, they ***make*** *you work very hard.*

To let = to allow.

Example:
In the Marines, they ***let*** *you go home for Christmas.*

The structure of both these verbs is the same:
Make/let + personal pronoun + infinitive without *to*.

	Present	Present continuous	Past simple
Affirmative	*He's exhausted.* ***Let*** *him rest.*	*I failed my exam, but they're* ***letting*** *me try again.*	*He was unhappy, so they* ***let*** *him leave the Marines.*
	The officers ***make*** *the trainees work hard.*	*These exercises are* ***making*** *me feel tired*	*They* ***made*** *me get up very early.*
Negative	***Don't let*** *him rest.*	*They're* ***not letting*** *us watch TV tonight.*	*They* ***didn't let*** *us smoke at meal times.*
	They ***don't make*** *you give up smoking.*	*I'm sick, so they're* ***not making*** *me do the exercises.*	*They* ***didn't make*** *me get up early on Sundays.*

The picture shows a man in the jungle.

In pairs, discuss:

1 What is this man's job?
2 Life in the jungle is difficult. What must he know?
3 What do you think these soldiers learn and do during their training?
4 Does this kind of job attract you? Why? Why not?

PRACTICE 1

A Make sentences, using these prompts. Begin with: *In the Marines…*

The first has been done for you:

1 get up/early (make)
In the Marines, they *make* you get up early.
2 take a lot of exercise (make)
3 smoke in the tea-break (let)
4 cut/hair (make)
5 wear uniform (make)
6 go home for Christmas (let)

B Fill the gaps below with *make* or *let*, as appropriate. Remember to change the verb form, if necessary.

The first one has been done for you:

My father is *letting* me borrow his car this evening.

1 In the school my father used to go to, they __________ him take cold showers.

2 Please __________ me go with you!

3 Can't you __________ that awful child be quiet?

4 Hurray! My boss is __________ me have a pay rise.

5 He didn't want to go into hospital, but the doctor __________ him go.

6 Don't __________ him have the front door keys. He isn't old enough.

VOCABULARY

Which words from Column A go with the words from Column B?

Column A	Column B
1 crawl	a cold
2 sleeping	b stones
3 climb	c on our hands and feet
4 sharp	d bag
5 freezing	e ropes

READING

a

b

A These pictures show some of the things they make you do during your training to be a Marine.

1 What are the trainees doing?

2 Do you think this kind of training is useful?

The following are extracts from the diary of Sandy Foster. He wrote them during a test training period with the Marines. Everything he describes is true.

1 Monday, 6 February

I feel really excited! Here I am at last! In the Commando Training Centre! There are thirty of us. Today was really difficult. It began with exercises. They made us do eighty-five sit-ups in two minutes, forty jumps in a minute, and run 300 metres in forty-one seconds... and that was just the start. Then it was the famous Tarzan Course – climbing ropes high in the air. If we fell off, they made us do it again, and again, and again...

2 Wednesday, 8 February

Well, there are only nineteen of us now. Today was even worse than yesterday or the day before. They made us crawl over sharp stones. They timed us, and because we didn't crawl fast enough, they made us do it again. I don't think I want to be a Commando any more. I just want to sleep and sleep. I feel so tired – they make us get up at 6.00 a.m., and they only let us have a ten-minute break in the morning, and an hour for lunch...

3 Friday, 10 February

There are only six of us left. Today they made us run for kilometres through mud. It was freezing cold. Then they made us walk for kilometres with heavy rucksacks on our backs.

4 Saturday, 11 February

I've never felt so cold and exhausted in my life. We can't even go to bed early in the evening, because we have to wash and iron all our clothes, and if we don't do it properly they make us get up at 4.00 a.m. and do exercises in the freezing cold. I'm so tired I want to die.

5 Monday, 13 February

I passed! I got through it! Me and one other guy, out of the thirty who started! Now we can really begin our training. I can do it – I'm going to be a Marine.

6 Tuesday, 30 October

We've just done Exercise Hunter's Moon. They left us alone in the mountains with a sleeping bag and some fish hooks. They didn't let us take any food, drink, cigarettes or money, but they did let us take some toilet paper! After two days, they gave us a live rabbit each. I was so cold and hungry that I made myself kill it. It was delicious! Maybe life as a Marine isn't so bad – they're letting us have a couple of weeks off for Christmas and then soon I shall be a Commando!

B Match the photographs to the paragraphs.

C Now read the diary extracts again, and answer these questions:

1 Was Sandy happy to begin his test training with the Marines?
2 How did his feelings change, and why?
3 What did they make him do on the first day?
4 How long did they let him have for lunch?
5 When did they make him get up?
6 What did they make him do on the Friday?
7 How many trainees passed the test training?
8 What did they let him take on Exercise Hunter's Moon?
9 What did Sandy make himself do?
10 Are they letting the trainees go home for Christmas?

PRACTICE 2

Now ask and answer questions about Sandy, using these prompts to help you.

The first has been done for you:

What/make/first day?

Question *What did they make him do on the first day?*
Answer *They made him do exercises and climb ropes.*

1 When/make/get up?
2 Where/make/crawl?
3 Did/make/ wash his clothes?
4 Where/make/run?
5 How far/make/walk/heavy rucksack?
6 Did/let/cigarettes/Exercise Hunter's Moon?
7 What/make himself do?
8 Do/let/trainees/home/Christmas?

WRITING

Use Sandy's diary extracts as a guide. Write a diary extract about either the happiest day of your life, or the most miserable – or both!

DEVELOPMENT

In pairs, talk about your time at school or in military service.

What did they *make/let* you do? (Think about the work, the food, the sleeping accommodation and leisure time.)

START UP

PART B

In pairs, look at the cartoon, and answer the following questions.

1 Why is the little man trying to interrupt the other soldier?
2 Why isn't the big soldier listening?
3 Do you often interrupt people? Why?
4 What do you say if someone interrupts you?

Function Focus

Interrupting

It isn't always polite to interrupt people, but there are times when it's necessary.
Here are some of the things we can say when we want to interrupt people, and some of the things we can say when people try to interrupt us!

Interrupting	Preventing interruptions
But...	*I'm afraid I haven't quite finished.*
I'm sorry to interrupt you, but...	*I haven't quite finished.*
Excuse me, could I say something here?	*Just let me finish, please...*
Can I say something, please?	*Just a minute.*
I'm sorry, but...	*Hold on a minute.*
Yes, but...	

PRONUNCIATION

Listen and repeat.

LISTENING

You will hear an interview between a journalist and the head of training in the Marines. The two men often interrupt each other.

A **As you listen, look at the Function Focus above, and put a tick by any of the phrases that you hear.**

B **This is the page of notes the interviewer prepared for the interview. He asked the questions in a different order from his notes. Listen again and write down the order he asked the questions in. Write 1–6 in the boxes. The first question is (d).**

a. Training time too short ☐
b. Money ☐
c. Trainers give trainees a bad time ☐
d. Only 15% applicants become Marines 1
e. Teaches aggression ☐
f. Training much too hard – fully clothed into icy water. ☐

DEVELOPMENT

1 What are the advantages and disadvantages of a career in the army?
2 Do you agree with the interviewer that life as a soldier is much too hard?
3 How does such a career compare with other careers in, for example, commerce, industry, education, science, the arts?
4 Which career interests you most?

SELF-HELP

Silent Letters

Some letters are silent.

1 Silent *gh*:

high *sigh* *eight* *bright* *night* *right*
sight *thought* *through* *weigh* *daughter*

But *gh* is pronounced as *f* in some words:

cough *laugh* *enough*

2 Silent *u*:

guard *guide* *guitar* *guest* *build*
biscuit

3 Silent *w*:

answer *wrong* *wrist* *write*

4 Silent *k*:

knee *know* *knife* *knot* *knowledge*

Look at the words above and underline the silent letters.

Then cover the notes above and underline the silent letters in the words below:

wrong *guard* *know* *biscuit* *cough*
write *knot* *daughter* *sight* *answer*
weigh *wrist* *enough* *bright*

VOCABULARY BANK

freezing cold *to climb* *to crawl* *to interrupt*
to let someone do something *to make someone do something* *to pass (a test)* *to take exercise*
to train

UNIT 25

PART A

START UP

The picture above illustrates the following supernatural beings:

1 a witch
2 a ghost
3 a fairy
4 a vampire
5 an angel

In pairs:

1 Match the supernatural beings in the picture to the list.
2 In your country, what sort of good or evil beings did people use to believe in?
3 Do you believe in supernatural beings? Why? Why not?

PRACTICE

A The followings sentences are about what people used to believe, and how they used to protect themselves from evil.

The sentences have been jumbled up. Some are questions and some are statements. Unjumble them!

1 from evil? / protect themselves / use to / How did people
2 wear necklaces / They used to / of garlic
3 the sign of the cross / to make / on their doors / They used
4 to believe? / did they / What / use
5 through the air / to think witches / They used / flew
6 the blood of young girls / They used to believe / vampires drank
7 to women they thought were witches? / they use to do / What did
8 alive / used to / burn them / They

B The pictures on page 99 show ghosts and spirits from different parts of the world.

In pairs, discuss which countries the ghosts and spirits come from.

Example:

Well, it might be an Indian ghost, but I don't think so, because...
It may be British, but I'm not sure.

1

2

3

LISTENING

In the dialogue, you will hear a conversation between Mrs Neville, the landlady of a pub called The Bird Cage, and one of her customers. She is telling him about the ghost they have in The Bird Cage.

A Listen and mark these statements true (T) or false (F):

		T	F
1	The landlady doesn't believe in ghosts.		
2	The customer doesn't believe in ghosts.		
3	The ghost is the ghost of a doctor.		
4	The landlady has never seen the ghost.		
5	The landlady spent the whole night in the room at the top of the house.		
6	The townspeople made a leper stay in that room.		
7	They let his family visit him.		
8	The leper killed himself.		

B

Interruptions

Listen to the dialogue again. The customer often interrupts the landlady. Write down the phrases he uses to interrupt her. How does she respond?

C First read this passage from the story and fill each gap with *make* or *let* and one of these verbs:

live *see* *stay* *hear* *leave* *go*

He was a leper. Anyway, the people of the town (1) __________ the man __________ in this little room. They kept him there and they (2) __________ him __________ his wife or children. They (3) __________ him __________ there for four years. He got worse, and knocked and knocked on the door to (4) __________ somebody __________ . At last, they (5) __________ him __________ the room. They told him they would (6) __________ him __________ home to see his family again. But when he got into the street he didn't see his family. He saw all the townspeople with stones in their hands. They stoned the poor man to death. No wonder his ghost is so unhappy.

DEVELOPMENT

What ghosts have you heard of or seen? Tell a ghost story to your partner.

READING

PART B

Some people like ghosts. Inn-keepers, for example, are very glad to have a ghost in the house, because supernatural beings attract tourists. Here are some real stories about ghosts, from a book about the ghosts and pubs of Britain.

A Read the stories, and match them to the titles below:

1 Murdered for Money
2 Mad Maude
3 The Riverside Ghost

A The Ferry Inn at Horning is on the river. The ghost at the Ferry Inn appears every twenty-two years. It is the ghost of a beautiful young girl. She was killed in one of the rooms there, many years ago, and the murderers threw her body into the river.

The landlord has seen the ghost. He said that on 25 September 1956, he was sitting in the inn at about midnight. He fell asleep, and then he suddenly woke up.

'I heard a noise,' he reported, ' and then I saw her, about three metres away. She was climbing the stairs. She was about twenty-five. She was very thin, and she was wearing a green dress. Her face was beautiful but deathly white.'

The landlord tried to speak to her, but she went towards the front door and disappeared through it. He opened the door, and looked out. The ghost was near the river. Then she disappeared into it.

B Nicholas Price is the owner of West Manor Hotel, near Oxford. He told me:

'I have been here eight years and I am sure there are three ghosts in this building. Our most famous ghost is Mad Maude. She was a woman with red hair. Some people thought she was a witch. She was burnt alive here about five hundred years ago. A lot of our visitors have seen or felt something. Maude is usually sitting down crying when people see her, late in the evenings. One year we had twenty-five American ghost-hunters to stay, but she didn't show up that night. I think she's a little shy.

C Peter Fry is the landlord of the The Plough at Holford. The ghost in this pub is that of a tall Spanish traveller who stayed there a long time ago. People thought he was carrying a lot of gold. When he left his room robbers killed him on the stairs. The robbers then broke into his room, but found nothing. Maybe he buried the money in the garden.

The ghost only appears during November. Peter told me:

'I have not seen him myself, but my wife and daughter have. My wife saw him standing in an upstairs room, a dark figure which disappeared after a few seconds. The next November, twelve months later, my daughter saw him too.'

B **Read the stories again, and fill in the chart below:**

Name of pub	Description of ghost	Who saw it	When	What it was doing?
A				
B				
C				

PRONUNCIATION

When we show that we are interested in what someone is saying, we usually use a high-rise intonation pattern.

Example:

I saw a ghost last night.
Did ***you****?*

Listen and repeat.

WRITING

Now write your own ghost story! Use the stories you have just read as guides. Here are some ideas to help you:

The Place: *The Ship Inn.*

The ghost: *a sad, fair-haired boy.*

What happened to him: *he killed himself because his fiancée left him and went away with his best friend.*

When: *early mornings in April.*

SELF-HELP

Revision

If youoften read your English books and notes, you know that it is very helpful.

If you don't often look at your books, you can start now.

If you go over what you have learnt you will remember it much better.

People learn in different ways. Try some of these suggestions and find the ways that are best for you.

1 Plan your time. Decide how much time you can spend revising every week. Keep that time only for revision.
2 Sometimes you may find it better to repeat something you are not sure of. But sometimes you may find it better to begin something new.
3 Look at difficult things first, when you are not tired. Do the easy things later.
4 Look back through your Course Book and Study Book. When you see a Grammar Guide or Function Focus, cover the examples and remember as many as possible. Then uncover and check if you are right.
5 Work with a friend – that way you can ask each other questions and discuss problems.
6 Revise a little at a time and revise the last few units you studied.
7 Don't just read through the books and your notes. Do the exercises again.
8 Read some of the dialogues and exercises aloud.
9 Look at some pages of vocabulary just before going to sleep. You may remember it better.

VOCABULARY

customer *evil* *ghost* *supernatural*
to believe *to exist*

UNIT 26

PART A

START UP

The picture shows an Englishman who lived in the last century. He was a successful doctor, but he didn't live like other people. He was an eccentric – that is, a bit different, maybe a little bit mad.

In pairs:

1 Describe the picture. What is unusual about the way this Englishman lived?
2 Do you know anybody whose life style is different from other people's?
3 Are older people more eccentric than young people?
4 Are you at all eccentric? In what way?

Grammar Guide

Verbs of liking and disliking with the *-ing* form

We use many verbs to express what we like and dislike doing.
Here are some of them:

like dislike enjoy hate love mind can't stand
can't bear be keen on be fond of be crazy about

All of these verbs are used like this:

Subject +	Verb + (prep)	Verb+*ing*	(+ Object)
I	***like***	*cooking.*	
Frank	***hates***	*wearing*	*shoes.*
He	***was fond of***	*surprising*	*his friends.*

Now look at the interrogative form:

Do *you*	***like***	*cooking?*	
Does *Frank*	***hate***	*wearing*	*shoes?*
Was *he*	***fond of***	*surprising*	*his friends?*

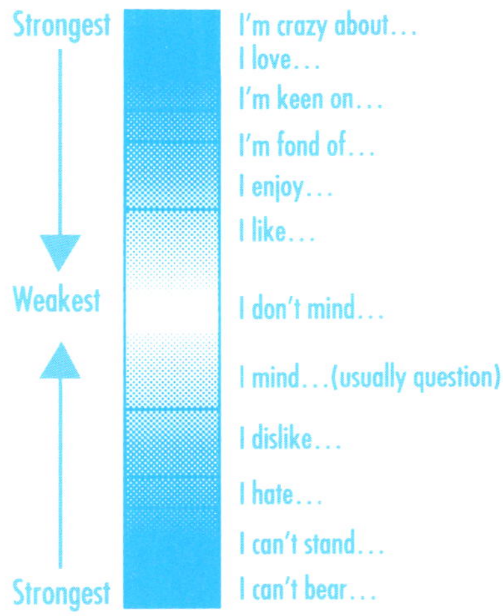

Verbs of Liking and Disliking

All these verbs are followed by either a noun or another verb with the *ing* form.
Some of these verbs have stronger meanings than others. This chart shows approximately how strong they are.
Note: The verb *mind* is usually used in negative and question form only.

PRACTICE

A Fill the gaps, using the following verbs:

1 I don't like (clean) __________ the bath.
2 I enjoy (ride) __________ my bicycle very much.
3 He loves (study) __________ foreign languages.
4 My cat hates (get) __________ wet.
5 They can't stand (go) __________ to parties.
6 She isn't very keen on (cook), __________ she loves (eat) __________ in restaurants.
7 He doesn't mind (walk) __________ to work.

B Choose the most appropriate verbs from the Grammar Guide to put in the gaps of the following sentences. In some of the sentences there is more than one possibility. Use the negative form if necessary.

The first has been done for you:

1 I __________ (go) __________ to the cinema; I go about twice or three times a month.
1 I *like going* to the cinema; I go about twice or three times a month.
2 Maria __________ (take) __________ photographs. She takes about forty pictures every day.
3 Christina __________ (go) __________ for walks, but she prefers doing something more active.
4 Alex __________ (be) __________ near cats. Whenever he sees one he gets ill.
5 Frank is a mathematician, so he __________ (do) __________ things like crosswords.
6 I __________ (write) __________ letters, so I usually telephone my friends.
7 What I __________ (do) __________ most of all is reading a good book in front of the fire.
8 Peter sometimes buys newspapers, but he __________ (read) __________ them.
9 Sally __________ (windsurf) __________ She goes whenever she can.
10 Well, actually, I'd prefer to go on foot. How about you – do you __________ (walk)?

DEVELOPMENT 1

In pairs make sentences using the verbs in the Grammar Guide, about things you like and dislike.

READING

These extracts are from a book about the world's most eccentric people.

Read these questions, then read the passages as quickly as you can, and answer the questions:

1 The picture at the beginning of the unit illustrates one of these stories. Which one?
2 Which eccentric hated meeting people?
3 Which two had strange eating habits?
4 One of them was very keen on keeping clean – which?
5 Which of the eccentrics was a sporting man?

A Howard Hughes was a billionaire. He loved watching films. He once spent three months in a room watching films night and day. He ate nothing but chocolate bars and nuts. He was crazy about flying as a child, and then made his money from aeroplanes. Later in life, he couldn't bear meeting people or touching things because he was afraid of germs. He covered his hands with a handkerchief before he touched anything. He hated cutting his hair or nails, which grew extremely long. In the fifteen years he spent hiding from other people, he only met three people from the outside world.

B John Mytton loved shooting, but he didn't like shooting with his clothes on. The only way he enjoyed shooting was without anything on – even in midwinter. He was also very fond of surprising his friends, and once arrived at a dinner party riding a brown bear. The bear then bit him in the leg and his host had to call a doctor.

C Frank Butland was born on 17 December, 1826. He loved animals. His house was full of live animals, most of them running free. His monkeys lived in the sitting room, and used to bite visitors. Frank gave them beer every night, and they were very fond of a drop of sweet wine on Sundays. He enjoyed cooking and eating a wide variety of animals. He often ate snake, and once made elephant's trunk soup. He boiled the trunk for several days, but it was too tough to eat. He ate rhinoceros, mice on buttered toast, kangaroos, giraffes and a bit of lion that died in a nearby zoo. The only thing he really disliked eating was flies. He hated wearing shoes and so he usually went barefoot. Frank said he got his strange tastes from his father, William, who ate a piece of Louis XIV's preserved heart.

D Beau Brummel enjoyed dressing. It took him three hours to arrange his tie, and his servants used champagne to polish his boots. He loved being clean, and spent two hours washing himself, morning and evening. He changed his shirt three times a day. He became engaged to a beautiful young woman, but broke the engagement when he discovered she ate cabbage. Beau hated eating vegetables of any kind.

DEVELOPMENT 2

In pairs.

Student 1 You are one of the above characters. Choose which one.
Student 2 Interview Student 1 about his/her likes and dislikes for an article in a newspaper about eccentrics and their lifestyles. Find out why Student 1 likes or dislikes the things he/she does.
Student 1 Give Student 2 as much information as you can.
Student 2 Take notes. When you have finished, change roles.

WRITING

Use the stories as a guide. Write a short newspaper article about the life-style of the person you interviewed.

PART B

START UP

1

2

In pairs, discuss:

Who are the people in the photographs and what do they have in common?

A lot of famous people are a little eccentric. Salvador Dali, the great Spanish surrealist painter, for example, led a very strange life, and Michael Jackson, the American pop singer, is a bit eccentric.

In pairs, discuss:

1 What do you know of the lives of these or other famous eccentrics?
2 What famous people from your country are a little eccentric?

Function Focus

Agreeing and Disagreeing with Affirmative and Negative Statements

When we want to talk about a shared opinion or experience, we can use these phrases:

Agreeing with affirmative statements:
I love swimming
I do, too / so do I / me too.
I'm very fond of dancing.
I am, too/so am I/me too.

Agreeing with negative statements:
I don't like driving.
I don't either/Neither do I.
I'm not very keen on going out tonight.
I'm not either/neither am I.

Disagreeing with affirmative statements:
I love swimming.
Do you? I don't.
I'm very fond of dancing.
Are you? I'm not.

Disagreeing with negative statements:
I don't like driving.
Don't you? I do.
I'm not very keen on going out tonight.
Aren't you? I am.

PRACTICE

Write two responses (one agreeing and one disagreeing) to the following statements, using the phrases above:

The first one has been done for you.

1 I love riding.
So do I/Do you? I don't.
2 I hate getting up early.
3 I don't like walking in the rain.
4 I'm very fond of spending my holidays in the sun.
5 I enjoy speaking English.
6 I dislike eating on my own in restaurants.
7 I don't mind doing the washing-up.
8 I'm not very keen on mountain climbing.
9 I dislike Monday mornings.
10 I don't mind going by bus.

LISTENING

Most people have something in particular that they dislike doing – maybe getting up early or waiting in queues. We call these things 'pet hates'.

A Some friends are discussing their pet hates. Listen to the dialogue and answer the following questions:

1 How many people are talking? Two or three?
2 Are they enjoying themselves?
3 Are the speakers students or working women?
4 Do they all hate paying taxes?
5 Do they hate going to the cinema?

B Read the list of pet hates. Listen to the cassette again and put a tick by the pet hates the speakers mention:

1 cleaning the bath
2 queueing for the bus
3 cooking cabbage
4 cleaning fish
5 being late
6 going for interviews
7 going to see their bank manager
8 paying tax
9 queueing for the cinema
10 having to wear smart clothes to work
11 playing sports
12 going to the dentist
13 doing exams
14 eating out alone
15 meeting people
16 getting up early
17 cleaning the lavatory

C Now underline your pet hates. You will need this for the Development exercise.

PRONUNCIATION

On the tape you will hear some phrases we use to agree and disagree with each others' opinions and experiences.

Listen and repeat.

DEVELOPMENT

In pairs, discuss your pet hates, and the pet hates of members of your family and friends. Use the list to give you ideas. Discuss in pairs, and give your opinions and experiences.

VOCABULARY BANK

life style *to bear* *to be crazy about*
to dislike *to be fond of* *to hate*
to be keen on *to mind*

UNIT 27

PART A

START UP

This is a picture of a television quiz show.

1 Do you enjoy watching shows like this? Why? Why not?
2 What kind of questions do people ask in these shows?
3 What are the best-known quiz shows in your country?
4 What sort of people take part in the shows?

Grammar Guide

Relative Clauses

A relative clause can be used to describe something or someone.
Example:
*The man **who is wearing glasses** is a pop singer.*

This is how we make a clause:
The man is a pop singer. + He is wearing glasses
who
*The man **who is wearing glasses** is a pop singer.*
Who is wearing glasses tells us something about the man.

Relative clauses for describing – *who, which.*

Who
Who is used to describe people.

Look at these sentences.
All the words in **bold** are used to describe the man or woman.
*The **tall** woman is a star.*
The word *tall* is an adjective.

Now look at this sentence:
*The **tall, pink-haired** woman **who is smiling** is a star.*
The words *tall, pink-haired* are adjectives, and the words *who is smiling* are a relative clause.

Which
Which is used to describe things.
*The suit **which he is wearing** is made of silk.*

Prepositions in relative clauses
When we use multi-word verbs in relative clauses we usually put the preposition at the end of the clause:
*The show **which they are taking part in** is a quiz show.*

PRACTICE

Work in pairs.

Student 1 Look at the picture at the beginning of the unit.

Student 2 Look at the picture on page 126 of the Appendices.

Student 1 Ask Student 2 the names of the people in the picture and fill in the spaces. Use relative clauses, for example, *What is the name of the woman who is wearing a pink dress?* If you are not sure how to spell the name, ask: *How do you spell it?*

READING

In pairs, discuss the following quiz questions. Tick the correct answers:

1 Alexander the Great was the man who:
a built the Parthenon.
b became King of Macedonia.
c wrote *The Republic.*

2 Rasputin was the man who:
a influenced the Russian court.
b wrote famous fairy stories.
c discovered electricity.

3 Freud was the man who:
a invented the aeroplane.
b wrote books about psychology.
c painted the ceiling of the Sistine Chapel.

4 Hydrogen is the element which is:
a extremely light.
b very heavy.
c highly poisonous.

5 Louis XIVthe King who built the Palace of Versailles:
a became King when he was five years old.
b fell in love with Mme de Pompadour.
c married Marie Antoinette.

6 The year which the first submarine was tested in was:
a 1910.
b 1801.
c 1958.

WRITING

A Rewrite these sentences using a relative clause.

The sentences have been begun for you.

Example:
I took part in a competition last month. I won it.
I won the competition ***which*** *I took part in last month.*

1 I took two prizes away. They were beautiful.
The prizes ________________________________

2 I had to write six names down. These are the names.
These are ________________________________

3 Then I had to mix all the letters up. These are the letters.
These are ________________________________

4 Finally I made up a sentence. It began with 'Holidays'.
I made ________________________________

B Write your own quiz. First look at the quiz questions in the Reading exercise again. In groups, discuss the quiz questions. Write them and give them to your teacher, who will be quiz-master.

PART B

START UP

In pairs, look at the cartoon:

1 What is the woman doing?
2 What is the man saying?

Function Focus

We often use exclamations to show our feelings.

We always say '*Good luck*' to our friends if they are going to take part in a competition, take an exam or go for an interview.

If they do well, we say '*Well done!*'

If they do badly, we say '*Never mind, better luck next time.*'

PRACTICE

Look at this list of exclamations. Read the statements below, and choose an appropriate exclamation for each one.

a Congratulations!
b Good luck! I hope you win.
c Well done mastermind!
d Good luck! I hope you get it!
e Oh no! That's terrible!
f Never mind! Better luck next time!

1 I've got an interview tomorrow. I really want the job.
2 We've decided to get married.
3 I've lost my wallet.
4 I've just failed my driving test.
5 I won the quiz!
6 We're playing Manchester United tomorrow.

PRONUNCIATION

Listen and repeat.

Pay special attention to the intonation of the phrases.

VOCABULARY

You will hear some of these words in the listening exercise.

What are the opposites of the words underlined?

1 To pass an exam __________
2 To be top of the class __________
3 To win a competition __________
4 To be very confident __________
5 He's the best player in the team __________
6 I had really good luck __________

LISTENING

You will hear six short dialogues.

As you listen, fill in the chart.

Some boxes have been completed for you.

1 Are the speakers happy or unhappy? (Column A)
2 What are they talking to each other about? (Column B)
3 Write down one or more of the exclamations you hear. (Column C)

	Column A	Column B	Column C
1		championship	
2	*unhappy*		
3			*Congratulations!*
4			
5			
6			

DEVELOPMENT

In pairs, imagine you are the people in these pictures. Make short conversations using the illustrations as prompts.

1

2

3

SELF-HELP

There are lots of ways of remembering new words. You can look at the shape of the word, you can think about how the word sounds, you can think about what the word means, and maybe make a picture in your mind of what the word means.

Tests show that if you only look at a word, you will soon forget it. If you think about the sound, it will help you remember, but if you think about the meaning of a word you will remember it best. Learning is an active process. The more you think about something, the better you remember it. If you ask yourself or your teacher lots of questions about the words, grammar or functions you are learning, you will be able to remember much better. Study with lots of questions in your mind – ask yourself questions about everything you are studying.

Match up these phrases:

1 If you think about the meaning of a word,
2 If you just look at the word,
3 If you think about the sound of a word,

a you'll forget it easily.
b you'll remember it best.
c it'll help you remember.

VOCABULARY BANK

confident *congratulations!* *luck*
well done! *to fail* *to lose* *to win*

START UP

In pairs, look at the picture. Discuss the following questions:

1 How many hours do you spend watching television every day?
2 Which programmes do you like/dislike most?
3 What are the advantages and disadvantages of TV?

Grammar Guide

Reported Speech

In reported speech the tense usually changes although the meaning remains the same.

That is sometimes used, but more often left out.

Look at this chart:

Direct speech	**Reported speech**
Present simple *I watch TV every day.*	**Past simple** *He said (that) he watched TV every day.*
Future Simple *I'll switch it off.*	***Would* form** *She said (that) she would switch it off.*
Present Continuous *I'**m watching** the news.*	**Past Continuous** *He said (that) he **was watching** the news.*
***Going to*, present** *I'**m going to** watch the quiz.*	***Going to*, past** *She said (that) she **was going to** watch the quiz.*

Modal verbs usually follow the same rules, but there are some exceptions.

Can *You **can** eat in front of the TV.*	***Could*** *He said (that) I **could** eat in front of the TV.*
Should *You **should** buy a new TV.*	***Should*** *She said (that) I **should** buy a new TV.*
Must *We **must** pay our TV licence.*	***Had to*** *They said (that) they **had to** pay their TV licence.*

Note: The negative form of *must* doesn't change in reported speech.
Example:
*She said (that) I **mustn't** smoke.*

PRACTICE

The producer is the person who finances a film; the director is the person who makes it.

A Study these sentences in direct speech, and then write them in reported speech.

The first one has been done for you.

1 'I work for a television company,' said Jack.
Jack said he worked for a television company.
2 'We need more money,' said the film director.
3 'I'm starting to film in five minutes,' he said.
4 'The producer is giving a party on Friday,' she said.
5 'That quiz show is rubbish,' John said.
6 'You're going to be very rich one day,' said the director.
7 'I'm not going to work for him again,' I said
8 'You can rest for ten minutes,' said the director
9 'I should have more pay,' said the film star.
10 'The film won't be ready on time,' said the producer.

B You have just missed *The News* on the television, but your friend watched it. You ask your friend about :

1 taxes
2 the rail strike
3 Northern Ireland
4 the World Cup
5 the weather tomorrow

Read these extracts from *The News*.

What did your friend say to you?

Example:

1 *He said taxes were going up by 5 per cent.*

Tonight's news...

taxes are going up by 5 per cent...

the rail strike will start at 6.00 a.m. tomorrow...

there is going to be a meeting next month in Northern Ireland to discuss solutions to the problems...

the World Cup will take place in Barcelona this year...

tomorrow is going to be dry and sunny...

VOCABULARY

Column 1 lists different kinds of TV programmes.
Column 2 describes the programmes.

Match the two columns.

Column 1	**Column 2**
1 documentaries	**a** music programmes
2 comedies	**b** factual films about animals and plants
3 the news	**c** informal talks, usually with famous people
4 the weather	**d** non-fiction films based on real events
5 chat shows	**e** programmes about football, tennis, swimming and so on
6 soap operas	**f** programmes which make you laugh
7 nature programmes	**g** information about temperature, rainfall, cloud, sun and so on
8 concerts	**h** the latest events in the world and in your country
9 sports	**i** dramas, usually about family life, often weekly

LISTENING

A On the cassette you will hear extracts from a news programme. Listen and complete Columns 1 and 2.

Name	1 Occupation	2 Place	3 What they said
Mervyn Flynn		*near America*	*He said*
John Green	*researcher*		*He said*
Stephanie Sand			*She said she was going to divorce Steve*
Hetty Smith		*Bristol*	*She said*
Springer Levin	*boxer*		*He said*
Frank Payne			*He said*

B Listen to the news again, and complete Column 3.

C What did the people in the news actually say? Look at Column 3, and change the reported speech into direct speech.

PRONUNCIATION

A Listen:

If the words have the same vowel sound as the word *film*, tick Column A. If the words have the same vowel sound as the word *TV*, tick Column B.

	Column A (*film*)	Column B (*TV*)
1		
2		
3		
4		
5		
6		
7		
8		

B Listen and repeat.

C Think of words that contain these sounds, and write a list of at least eight. Do not show them to your partner. In pairs, read out the words on your list to your partner. Your partner must say A or B, as appropriate.

DEVELOPMENT

Look back at Column 1 of the Vocabulary exercise. In groups of three, discuss which of these kinds of programmes you like and dislike.

START UP

PART B

In pairs, look at the cartoon and discuss the questions:

1 Do you, or does anyone in your family, make home movies?

2 Do you enjoy watching home movies? Why? Why not?

3 Do you have a video recorder? What do you use it for?

Function Focus

Descriptions

Situation 1
You missed a TV programme you wanted to watch, so you ask a friend: *'What was it like?'*
Your friend replies: *'Terrible'.*

Situation 2
Your friend saw a new film last week. You ask him: *'What was it like?'*
Your friend replies: *'Terrific'.*

Which one did the friend think was good and which one was bad...?
Often when people ask us for an opinion about something we simply use a single word.
Here are some more words we can use:
brilliant awful ghastly terrific dreadful fantastic amazing wonderful terrible

PRACTICE

A These adjectives can be used to describe TV programmes.

Put them into the two columns. For example, *terrible* goes in the bad column.

Good	Bad
brilliant	*terrible*

Remember: We don't use *very* with these words because the meaning is already strong.

B These adjectives are not only used to describe television programmes. They can describe many different things, such as films, magazines, meals, books, football matches – almost anything, in fact.

Fill the gaps in these sentences with an appropriate adjective. Do not use the same adjective twice.

1 She told me the film was __________ , so I'm going to see it next weekend.
2 The weatherman said the weather would be __________ tomorrow. Let's go to the beach.
3 That programme about computers was absolutely __________ . John recorded it on video and he said I could borrow it if I liked.
4 My boss said that restaurant was really __________ . Don't go there!
5 Sam said he had to go home to bed. He said he felt __________ .
6 My teacher said the new sports centre was __________ . We have to go as soon as we can.
7 John didn't enjoy his holiday. He said the hotel was really __________ .
8 Can I see the photographs? Peter said they were __________ and he could give me copies if I wanted.

C **What did the people in part B actually say? Change the reported speech into direct speech, like this: *She told me the film was brilliant – She said: 'The film is brilliant.'***

READING

A Many people like watching films on the TV. These are some of the different types of film:

a comedy
b thriller
c love story
d science fiction film
e western

1

2

Look at the photographs above.

What type of film do they come from?

B **Read the reviews and match them to the film types *a–e***

1 *Camille Claudel – Passion in Paris* The true story of the love of Camille (Isabelle Adjani) for the sculptor Rodin (Gerard Dépardieu). Directed by Bruno Nuytten.
2 *Pale Rider* Starring Clint Eastwood in the film he wrote and directed himself. Perhaps one of the best classic cowboy films since *Shane.*
3 *Arthur 2: On the Rocks* Dudley Moore returns as the millionaire who likes a drink, with Liza Minelli and John Gielgud. Directed by Bud Yorkin. Quite funny, but not as good as *Arthur 1.*
4 *Tequila Sunrise* A fast-moving thriller about drug-smuggling and old friendships, stars Mel Gibson, Kurt Russell and lovely Michelle Pfeiffer as the woman in the middle.
5 *Alien Nation* Sci-fi film from the producer of *Aliens.* Policeman James Caan joins with a partner from another world (Mandy Patikin of the Princess Bride) to chase the baddies.

C **Read the reviews again, and answer the following questions:**

1 Which actor directed his own film?
2 Is *Arthur 2* better than *Arthur* 1?
3 What role does James Caan play in *Alien Nation*?
4 Who plays Rodin in *Camille Claudel*?
5 Who is the female star in *Tequila Sunrise*?

D **Re-read the reviews and arrange the films in the order of preference – starting with number 1 as the film you would most like to see, and number 5 as the film you would least like to see. Then in groups of three, decide which film to watch.**

VOCABULARY BANK

amazing awful brilliant dreadful
wonderful concerts film news
programme sports weather

UNIT 29

PART A

START UP

Look at this picture of a trial in a courtroom. Discuss the questions with your partner.

1 Which person is the judge? What does he do? Where is the jury, and what do they do?
2 What happens in a trial?
3 Re-arrange the following crimes in order of seriousness. The first will be the most serious, the fifth will be the least serious: kidnapping, drug selling, murder, drunk driving, burglary.

Grammar Guide

Question Tags

We usually use question tags when we want to check information.

Look at this:

Speaker 1 *You're from Hong Kong,* ***aren't you****?*
Speaker 2 *Yes I am.*

Speaker 1 is almost sure that Speaker 2 is from Hong Kong, but he/she wants to be completely sure.

Now look at the negative question tag:

Speaker 1 *You're not from Brazil,* ***are you****?*
Speaker 2 *No I'm not.*

Question tags are usually made up of the same auxiliary or modal verb and pronoun that are used in the main part of the sentence.

Look at these:

1 *You have told the police,* ***haven't you****?*
2 *We didn't persuade the judge,* ***did we****?*
3 *Robert's going to prison,* ***isn't he****?*
4 *They look nervous,* ***don't they****?*
5 *There can't be a mistake,* ***can there****?*

Note:

1 In Number 3 we don't repeat 'Robert' in the question tag, we use the pronoun.

2 In Number 4 we can't see the auxiliary (do), but we can see it in the question tag (don't they?).

PRONUNCIATION 1

With these question tags, the intonation falls at the end of the sentence.

Listen and repeat.

VOCABULARY

Match this list of words to the meanings below:

a criminal
b prison
c fine
d prisoners
e judge

1 Money you have to pay as a punishment.
2 The man who decides the punishment.
3 The place where criminals are locked away.
4 People who stay in prisons.
5 Someone who breaks the law.

PRACTICE

Write the question tags for these sentences:

1 He's a famous criminal, __________ ?
2 He hasn't been to prison, __________ ?
3 The police caught him, __________ ?
4 He should pay a fine, __________ ?
5 There's no proof, __________ ?
6 The judge will be very angry, __________ ?
7 Most criminals make trouble, __________ ?
8 He might be set free, __________ ?
9 The prisoner's going home today, __________ ?
10 You're the judge, __________ ?

PRONUNCIATION 2

Now you will hear the same sentences again. Listen and repeat them.

DEVELOPMENT

In pairs, write down some of the things you know about your partner, such as where he/she lives, his/her age, people in his/her family, where he /she went on holiday last year, things he/she has bought, exams he/she has passed, plans for the future and so on.

Now check all the information you have written down, by asking your partner questions with question tags.

READING

A There was a burglary at 7.30 p.m. on the evening of 9 September. The police thought Paul Lighthand, a well-known criminal, was the burglar. They found him and asked him what he was doing on that night. This is what he told them. Unfortunately, the policeman mixed up all the sentences.

Can you put the sentences in the right order?

1 Afterwards, I went out to the Red Lion for a drink. I met several friends, and spent the evening talking and playing cards.
2 There we met some girls and danced all night. I left the disco at 3.00 a.m. and took a girl home by taxi. I then returned to my own home, arriving at about 3.30 a.m.
3 I got back with the fish at about 8.00 p.m. I had my meal, and then I watched the *News at Nine*.
4 On the evening of Sunday, 9 September, I came back from work at about 7.00 p.m. I switched the television on and made myself some tea.
5 I sat and watched *Dynasty* on TV for half an hour, and then I went out to get some fish and chips at the 'Flying Fish'.
6 The pub closed at 11.00 p.m. and we went on to a disco, the 'Alcatraz'.

B **Now read the passage again and fill in the chart.**

Look at the example:

Time	Actions
7.00 7.30	*Went to get fish and chips.*
8.00	
9.00	
11.00	
3.00 3.30	*Got home.*

In pairs, look at the cartoon.

After the robbery the people in the picture talked about it. Who said what?

1 It was a terrible failure.
2 Well, it was a change from routine.
3 We had a big surprise at the bank this morning.
4 It was an easy arrest.
5 My cashier was wonderful.

a the Police
b the robber
c the bank manager
d customer at the bank
e the cashier

Function Focus

Checking Information

Question tags are one way of checking information. Now let's look at some others:

You mean...?	***You mean** you watched TV for half an hour?*
What do you mean?	
So you/he...?	***So you** went to the coffee bar, not the fish and chip shop?*
Are you quite sure...?	***Are you quite sure** you watched Dallas?*
Are you certain?	***Are you certain** of that?*
Is that right?	*You left home at about 9 o'clock, **is that right**?*
Can you explain ...?	***Can you explain** why you got home at 3.30 a.m?*
Can you explain that?	

LISTENING

A You will hear part of what happened in the courtroom, at Mr Lighthand's trial. A lawyer is questioning Mr Lighthand.

Listen to the cassette. Compare what Mr Lighthand says in court to what he told the police on page 115. How does he change his story? (Three things are different.)

B **Listen again, and in the Function Focus tick any of the phrases you hear.**

C **Listen once more, and fill in the gaps:**

1 And you went inside and __________ a cup of coffee, __________ you?
2 And then you __________ the television – __________ *Dynasty*, __________ it?
3 So you definitely __________ *Dallas* on that Wednesday evening, __________ ?
4 You __________ television at all on Wednesday evening, __________ ?
5 Mr Lighthand, you __________ or in a chip shop on Wednesday evening, __________ ?

DEVELOPMENT

Work in pairs.

Student 1 You are a policeman,
Student 2 You are a well-known criminal.

The police think that a criminal (Student 2) robbed a bank on Thursday morning, the 22 March. They have caught him/her (Student 2).

A

Student 1 Prepare questions to ask Student 2 about what he/she did/was doing on the morning of the robbery, for example, *'When did you get up, what were you doing at 10.00 a.m. in the morning?'* and so on.

Student 2 Prepare a detailed explanation of everything you did that morning.

B

Student 1 Question Student 2 in detail about what he/she did on the day of the robbery. Get as much information as you can. Check the facts to make sure that you get the story right.Take notes of Student 2's replies. You will need these in the next exercise.

Student 2 Give as much information as you can to Student 1.

WRITING

Using the notes that you took in the Development exercise, write up a report of what Student 2 did on the morning of the robbery.

VOCABULARY BANK

criminal *judge* *prison* *prisoner* *robbery*
trail *to fine* *to judge*

UNIT 30

PART A

START UP

You Have Won £ 1,000,000!

In pairs discuss:

1 How you won the money.
2 What you think you will do with it.
3 What is the best way to get rich quickly: doing football pools, betting on horses, buying shares in the stockmarket, setting up your own business, robbing a bank, treasure hunting, marrying a rich man or woman.
4 Do you want to be rich? Why?

1

2

READING

A These pictures are of people who have become very rich very quickly. How do you think they did it?

B These stories of the people in the pictures have come from a magazine article.

Read them, and match the passages to the illustrations.

A Celia Tynan wrote her first novel when she was almost forty. It was a bestseller all over the world. Celia is a single mother, and before she wrote the book, she could not make enough money for herself and her daughter to live on.

She spent a year writing the novel, in a corner of her bedroom.

She has signed a contract for her next novel, with an advance of £300,000. She thinks each novel she writes earns her between half a million and a million pounds. Having money has not changed her lifestyle very much, but it has taken away all her financial worries:

'(1) I enjoy writing. I never think about money now. I'm much more relaxed and happy.'

And the future?

'(2) I don't want to work so hard because I want to spend more time with my daughter.'

B Jackie Butcher won £300,000 on the football pools. She and her husband bought two houses, a lot of shares, and gave some money to charities. Jackie is going to keep her job as a shop-keeper, but says:

'(3) It's lovely to shut the shop and go on holiday whenever we want. But a lot of customers aren't buying things from our shop anymore. Those customers think we don't need any more money.'

And the future?

'(4) I like buying expensive shoes, so now I can buy as many as I like, and I'm going to buy a pony for my daughter.'

C Four years ago, Simon May was very poor. Then he wrote the theme music for a TV soap opera called *Eastenders*. The theme music took him three minutes to write. Now *Eastenders* is sold all over the world, and the music has been recorded by several well-known groups and singers. Since then Simon has written the theme music for another TV soap opera, *Howard's Way*, and the work keeps coming in.

'(5) I'm very lucky, but my sudden wealth isn't going to change my life. I don't drive an expensive car, and I still make two cups of tea with one teabag.'

D Steve Knight used to play a word game with his friends at university. To play the game, you ask each other questions like: *'If he were a car, what sort of car would he be?' 'If she were an animal, what sort of animal would she be?'* Steve is now twenty-nine, and this game has made him more money than he ever dreamed. He sold it to games companies in the UK and America, and they paid the biggest advance ever for an untried board game.

'(6) The deal for the British sales alone will be four or five million over the next few years, and my share of that is one third.'

He is hoping to buy a house in Spain, but not an expensive car or clothes.

'(7) None of my friends seem jealous of me – if anything, people are nicer to me now that I'm successful.'

PRACTICE

These sentences are in direct speech in the magazine article. Change them into reported speech, and fill in the gaps. The sentences are numbered 1–7.

1 Celia Tynan said __________ and she never __________ now. She added __________ much more relaxed and happy.
2 She said __________ so hard because she __________ more time with her daughter.
3 Jackie Butcher said that __________ and go on holiday __________ but she added that a lot of customers __________ from their shop any more. She said those customers thought __________ .
4 She said __________ buying expensive pairs of shoes, so now __________ as many as she liked and she added that she __________ a pony for her daughter.
5 Simon May said __________ , but he added that all his sudden wealth __________ life. He said he __________ an expensive car and he still __________ two cups of tea with one tea bag.
6 Steve Knight said that the deal for British sales alone __________ for four or five million over the next few years, and that his share __________ .
7 He said that none of his friends __________ , and that, if anything, people __________ nicer to him now.

LISTENING

On the cassette you will hear a businessman talking to a group of students who are following a course in Business Studies. The subject of his talk is, 'Getting Rich doing Business'.

A **Read the statements and listen. Mark them true (T) or false (F) with a tick:**

		T	F
1	Making your first million is difficult.		
2	Making your second million is easy.		
3	The late J. Paul Getty made his money in the aeroplane business.		
4	Howard Hughes was one of the richest men in the world.		
5	Laura Ashley began her business in a big way.		
6	Body Shop was set up by a bored housewife.		
7	Scandinavian countries have very high living standards.		
8	Scandinavian countries have low suicide rates.		

B **Listen again, and match these relative clauses to their main clauses to make sentences like those you hear:**

Main clauses	Relative clauses
1 Howard Hughes... ended his life frightened and alone.	**a** which began very small
2 The late J. Paul Getty...lived as a prisoner in his own home.	**b** who began printing fabrics in her kitchen
3 The Scandinavian countries...also have the highest suicide rate.	**c** which began in a small way too
4 Laura Ashley...had the right idea at the right time.	**d** who was a self-made oil millionaire
5 Body Shop...was set up by a bored housewife.	**e** which have the highest living standards in the world
6 A lot of businesses... are now worth millions.	**f** who was one of the richest men in the world

DEVELOPMENT

Self-Made Millionaires

A In groups discuss people you have heard of who have become rich – maybe athletes, business people, musicians.

1 What did they do?
2 How long did it take them to become rich?
3 Would you like to be one of these people? Which one?

B In pairs discuss some businesses and well-known business people in the country you come from.

WRITING

Write answers to the following questions. Use the prompts to help you. If you need help, look at the reading exercise at the beginning of the unit.

1 Who is Celia Tynan?	first novel/when she was almost forty
2 Who is Jackie Butcher?	£300,000 on the football pools
3 Who is Simon May?	theme music/TV soap opera
4 Who is Steve Knight?	sold a game/millions of pounds.

PART B

START UP

1

2

3

In pairs, look at these pictures:

Student 1 Make sentences using verbs of liking or disliking, for example, *I like swimming/I'm not very keen on cooking.*

Student 2 Respond like this: *I do too/so do I/do you? I don't/I'm not either/neither am I/aren't you? I am,* as appropriate.

PRACTICE 1

These are responses to statements. In pairs, think of appropriate statements and write them down.

The first one has been done for you:

1 Me too!
I love playing football/ I enjoy going to discos/ I like learning English.
2 So do I.
3 I don't either.
4 So am I.
5 I'm not either.
6 So did I.
7 I haven't either.
8 Neither can I.

PRACTICE 2

Ask yourself the questions below and fill in Column A of the grid. Now ask two of your classmates the questions, and fill in Columns B and C of the grid. Do they like/dislike doing the same things as you?

Example:

Speaker 1 *What do you enjoy doing in the evening?*
Speaker 2 *I like watching television.*
Speaker 1 *So do I.*

Speaker 1 *And what do you like doing at parties?*
Speaker 2 *I love dancing.*
Speaker 1 *Do you? I don't!*

Question	A Your name	B Name	C Name
1 What do you enjoy doing in the evening?			
2 What do you like doing at parties?			
3 What can't you stand doing on holiday?			
4 What are you keen on doing at weekends?			
5 What do you dislike doing at school/at work?			
6 What do you enjoy doing in winter?			

PRACTICE 3

Your friend says the following things to you. What situations might you be in?

The first one has been done for you.

1 Congratulations!

Situation: *You have just won a competition.*

2 Good luck! I hope you win.

Situation: ______________________

3 Well done!

Situation: ______________________

4 Good for you! That's terrific!

Situation: ______________________

5 Oh no! That's terrible!

Situation: ______________________

6 Never mind! Better luck next time!

Situation: ______________________

7 Good luck! I hope you get it!

Situation: ______________________

DEVELOPMENT

Discuss which parts of this book have been easy for you and which difficult.

1 Which kind of exercises did you enjoy least/most, and why?
2 What are the the most important things you have learnt since the start of the course?
3 Is there anything you still don't understand or you don't feel very sure about?
4 Is there anything you need to revise?

SELF-HELP

When you study English, you have to learn a lot of words. In Unit 20 of the Course Book, we saw that the good language learner develops techniques to help him/her learn. Do you use any techniques to help you remember ?

Try this exercise before you read on.

1 Look at the illustration below for one minute.
2 Cover the illustration and write down as many of the items as you can remember. If you don't know the word in English, write it in your own language.
3 Count how many you remembered.

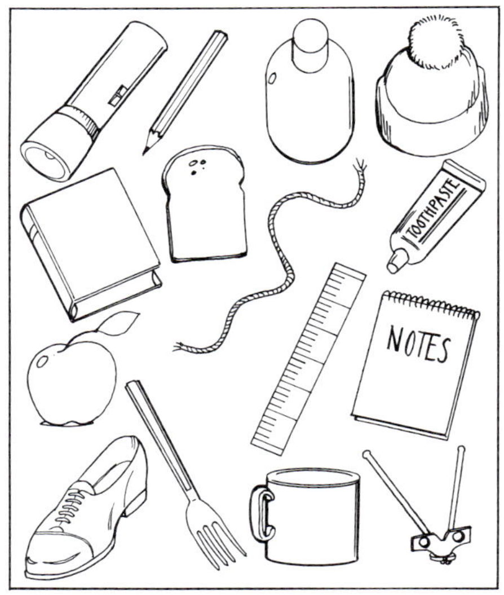

If you want to remember more, try this technique:

1 Look at one of the items.
2 Make a mental picture of it. Make the picture as funny or strange as possible.
3 Look at another of the items.
4 Connect the first item with the second item, by making a mental picture of the two items linked in some way.
5 Link a third item with the second, still making mental pictures. Continue like this for one minute, making a chain of items.
6 Cover the illustration and write down the list. You will find you remember much more easily and with greater certainty.
7 Practise the technique, and use it to help you learn English whenever you can.

VOCABULARY BANK

jealous *novel* *sales* *shares* *to earn*

IRREGULAR VERBS

Infinitive	Past	Past participle
be	was	been
beat	beat	beaten
begin	began	begun
break	broke	broken
bring	brought	brought
buy	bought	bought
catch	caught	caught
choose	chose	chosen
come	came	come
cost	cost	cost
dig	dug	dug
dream	dreamt	dreamt
drink	drank	drunk
drive	drove	driven
eat	ate	eaten
fall	fell	fallen
find	found	found
fly	flew	flown
forget	forgot	forgotten
get	got	got
give	gave	given
go	went	gone
have	had	had
hear	heard	heard
hide	hid	hidden
hold	held	held
keep	kept	kept
know	knew	known
lay	laid	laid
learn	learnt	learnt
leave	left	left
lend	lent	lent
let	let	let
lose	lost	lost
make	made	made
meet	met	met
pay	paid	paid
put	put	put
read	read	read
ride	rode	ridden
ring	rang	rung
run	ran	run
say	said	said
see	saw	seen
sell	sold	sold
send	sent	sent
shut	shut	shut
sing	sang	sung
sit	sat	sat
sleep	slept	slept
smell	smelt	smelt
speak	spoke	spoken
stand	stood	stood
steal	stole	stolen
swim	swam	swum
take	took	taken
teach	taught	taught
tear	tore	torn
tell	told	told
think	thought	thought
throw	threw	thrown
understand	understood	understood
wake	woke	woken
wear	wore	worn
win	won	won
write	wrote	written

APPENDIX 1: UNIT 6: PAGE 24

Student 2 This is a page from your diary. Some of your friends will talk to you to find out when you are free to go out with them.

Saturday	going to cousin's wedding in Scotland
Sunday	party at Ann's house
Monday	
Tuesday	mend the car, then dinner with Sally
Wednesday	
Thursday	Dallas on TV!
Friday	

Student 3 This is a page from your diary. Some of your friends will talk to you to find out when you are free to go out with them.

Saturday	painting my room, coffee with John 8.30pm
Sunday	
Monday	
Tuesday	meal with school friends
Wednesday	
Thursday	watch Dallas
Friday	do homework for next Monday

APPENDIX 2: UNIT 8: PAGE 33

the trousers: large, £20.99
the skirt: medium, £29.99
the scarf: one size, £5.50
the gloves: small, £15.00
the boots: medium, £67.50
the jacket: large, £20.00
the coat: small, £25.99
the shirt: medium, £15.25
the jumper: large, £23.00
the cardigan: small, £19.50

Student 2 You are the shop assistant. Your partner is a customer in your shop. He/she does not know the prices or sizes of the clothes. Do not show him/her the list above. Give your partner the information he/she asks for.

APPENDIX 3: UNIT 9: PAGE 37

Student 2 You are Tracy and you are asking the consultant for advice. Read about your problems before you begin to speak to the consultant, then explain your problems one by one. Respond to the suggestions the consultant makes – are they useful or not? What are the further problems that might occur if you follow the consultant's suggestions? You do not have to agree with the consultant!

Here are your problems:

1 One of your workers is stealing your clothes.
2 You aren't selling enough clothes to make a good profit.
3 You would like to become a bigger business, but you haven't enough money.
4 It takes you a long time to do your tax – and then you usually get it wrong.
5 You need to employ more people to help you.
6 You advertise occasionally, but it doesn't seem to do any good.
7 You've never got any money in the bank.

APPENDIX 4: UNIT 11: PAGE 45

FITZ HOTEL PERSONNEL RECRUITMENT FORM

PART A

Name: ____________ Age: ______

Address: ____________

Telephone: ____________

Skills: ____________

Experience: ____________

Present Job: ____________

PART B

1. School: ____________
2. Exams: ____________
3. Languages: ____________
4. Length of time in present job: ____________
5. Number of jobs since College: ____________
6. Experience in hotel work: Yes ____ No ____
7. Details: ____________

APPENDIX 5: UNIT 13: PAGE 52

Susi ...Yes, but you can learn English at a school in your own country much more (1) __________ than in the UK.

Marie That's true, but you can study in a language school in the UK more (2) __________ than at home.

Susi What do you mean?

Marie Well for one thing the teachers in the UK can teach (3) __________ .

Susi That's not true. We've got very good teachers at home, and you can even see English films and buy English newspapers.

Marie Yes, but I think you learn (4) __________ in Britain.

Susi Maybe you learn more quickly, but it costs you more.

Marie Yes, you're right, but you can work as an au-pair. Then you're paid to learn English.

Susi That's nonsense. You're paid to do the housework and look after the children and you work (5) __________ than in an ordinary job.

Marie Perhaps, but you learn English (6) __________ and you make friends with British people more (7) __________ .

Susi Hmm. It sounds quite a good idea. Tell me more.

Marie Well, you work quite (8) __________ – about thirty hours a week, and you must be twenty-five or younger. You aren't paid very (9) __________ – only about £30.00 a week, but you do get free board and lodging.

APPENDIX 6: UNIT 16: PAGE 63

Student 1 You are Sybil Smith. A radio interviewer is asking you about the meaning of dreams. Look at the information below, and answer the interviewer's questions. Make sentences such as: *If you dream about a banana, you'll have an unhappy marriage.* The interviewer will ask you about some dreams which are not in the list below. Use your imagination!

Dream	**Meaning**
leaves	a happy journey
banana	unhappy marriage
fish	bad health
a wallet	difficulties
children	good luck
bottles	good luck in love

B

Western Bank Plc Service application form

Mr, Mrs, Ms

Initials

Surname

Address

Tel no　　Postcode

Foreign currency notes

Country	Amount of foreign currency	or	Sterling equivalent

Sterling travellers cheques

Available for use in all countries throughout the world, but travellers in North and Latin America and the Philippines are advised to take travellers cheques expressed in US Dollars

Name of person signing cheques

Number required		Value
	of £10 each	
	of £20 each	
	of £50 each	
	of £100 each	

Declaration

Please delete as appropriate

-Please debit my account number

Account holding branch

-I undertake to provide payment by: Access/Visa/Mastercard/American express/Diners card

Account name

Card number

Customer signature

Date

APPENDIX 8: UNIT 23: PAGE 91

a Madame Canals 1905. A study of a woman. She is wearing a black scarf, and there is a flower in her hair. Picasso.

b The Entombment, about 1495. Several figures with the dead Christ at the centre of the picture. Michelangelo.

Student 2 Look at this picture. Do not show it to your partner. Your partner will ask you about the names of the people in the picture. Tell your partner their names, using relative clauses to describe the people, for example, *The man who is wearing a suit and glasses is Elton John.* You will have to spell some of the names to your partner.